LARSON
ALGEBRA 2

COMMON CORE State Standards
Curriculum Companion

Student Edition

Ron Larson

Laurie Boswell

Timothy D. Kanold

Lee Stiff

HOLT McDOUGAL

HOUGHTON MIFFLIN HARCOURT

Larson Algebra 2
Common Core State Standards
Curriculum Companion
Student Edition

Contents

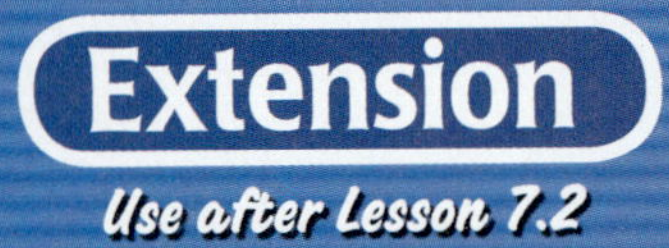

Transform Expressions of Exponential Functions

GOAL Use properties of exponents to rewrite exponential functions.

By rewriting exponential growth and decay functions, you can understand more completely the real-life situations that these functions model.

EXAMPLE 1 Rewrite an exponential growth function

MUSIC SALES From 2004 to 2010, the number y (in millions) of songs sold by an online music store can be modeled by $y = 100(1.08)^t$ where t is years since 2004. Find the approximate monthly percent increase in sales.

Solution

Because t is given in years and $1.08 = 1 + 0.08$, the annual percent increase is 8%. To find the monthly percent increase that gives an 8% annual increase, use the fact that $t = \frac{1}{12}(12t)$ and the properties of exponents to rewrite the model in a form that reveals the monthly growth rate.

$$y = 100(1.08)^t \qquad \text{Write original function.}$$

$$= 100(1.08)^{(1/12)(12t)} \qquad t = \left(\frac{1}{12}\right)(12t)$$

$$= 100(1.08^{1/12})^{12t} \qquad \text{Power of a power property}$$

$$\approx 100(1.0064634)^{12t} \qquad \text{Evaluate power.}$$

> **CHECK UNDERSTANDING**
> $1.08^{1/12}$ is the 12th root of 1.08, so the 12th power of the 12th root of 1.08 is 1.08.

To check the rewritten model, notice that $t = 1$ gives $100(1.006434)^{12} \approx 108$, which is the same result as for the original model with $t = 1$. The monthly increase in sales is about 0.0064, or 0.64%.

EXAMPLE 2 Rewrite an exponential decay function

MEDICAL DIAGNOSTICS The amount A (in grams) remaining of n grams of the radioactive isotope chromium-51 after t days is given by $A = n\left(\frac{1}{2}\right)^{t/28}$. What percent of the chromium-51 decays each day?

Solution

Use the fact that $\frac{t}{28} = \left(\frac{1}{28}\right)t$ to rewrite the model in a way that reveals the daily growth rate.

$$A = n\left(\frac{1}{2}\right)^{t/28} \qquad \text{Write original function.}$$

$$= n\left[\left(\frac{1}{2}\right)^{1/28}\right]^t \qquad \text{Power of a power property}$$

$$\approx n(0.9755)^t \qquad \text{Evaluate power.}$$

$$= n(1 - 0.0245)^t \qquad \text{Rewrite in form } y = a(1 - r)^t.$$

▶ The daily decay rate is about 0.0245, or 2.45%.

FINANCE What annual interest rate is needed for the balance of an account to double every 15 years?

Solution

STEP 1 Write an exponential function for the amount A in the account after t years when the principal (original amount) is P. Notice the following:

When $t = 15$: $\quad A = P \cdot 2^1 = P \cdot 2^{15/15}$

When $t = 30$: $\quad A = P \cdot 2^2 = P \cdot 2^{30/15}$

When $t = 45$: $\quad A = P \cdot 2^3 = P \cdot 2^{45/15}$

In general, the amount in the account after t years is $A = P(2)^{t/15}$.

STEP 2 Rewrite the function to find the annual interest rate.

$$A = P(2)^{t/15} \qquad \text{Write original function.}$$

$$= P(2^{1/15})^t \qquad \text{Power of a power property}$$

$$\approx P(1.0473)^t \qquad \text{Evaluate power.}$$

$$= P(1 + 0.0473)^t \qquad \text{Rewrite in form } y = a(1 + r)^t.$$

▶ The annual interest rate needed is about 0.0473, or 4.73%.

PRACTICE

EXAMPLES 1 AND 2
on p. CC2
for Exs. 1–4

1. ELECTRICITY For an 8 week period beginning June 1, the amount y (in kilowatt-hours) of electricity used by a business was approximately $y = 750(1.02)^t$ where t is the number of weeks since June 1. What daily percent increase in electricity use does this model represent?

2. HALF-LIFE The amount y (in grams) remaining of n grams of the radioactive isotope sodium-24 after t hours is given by $A = n\left(\frac{1}{2}\right)^{t/15}$. Find the hourly decay rate.

3. TECHNOLOGY A new computer system costs $2400. The value of the computer system decreases by 28% each year. Find the daily percent decrease in the value of the computer.

4. REAL ESTATE From 2000 to 2010, median home prices in Austin, Texas, rose an average of 7.2% per year. Find the monthly percent increase in the value of a home in Austin during 2000–2010.

EXAMPLE 3
on p. CC3
for Exs. 5–6

5. FINANCE Find the annual interest rate needed for the balance of an account to double every 10 years.

6. MARINE BIOLOGY The population of a species of phytoplankton doubles every 3 days. Find the daily percent increase in the population.

7. WRITING Suppose you are given the number of years it takes for a quantity to double. *Describe* how to find the annual rate of increase of the quantity without writing a function that models the situation.

Mastering the Standards

for Mathematical Practice

The topics described in the Standards for Mathematical Content will vary from year to year. However, the *way* in which you learn, study, and think about mathematics will not. The Standards for Mathematical Practice describe skills that you will use in all of your math courses.

Mathematical Practices

1. *Make sense of problems and persevere in solving them.*
2. *Reason abstractly and quantitatively.*
3. *Construct viable arguments and critique the reasoning of others.*
4. *Model with mathematics.*
5. *Use appropriate tools strategically.*
6. *Attend to precision.*
7. *Look for and make use of structure.*
8. *Look for and express regularity in repeated reasoning.*

1 Make sense of problems and persevere in solving them.

Mathematically proficient students start by explaining to themselves the meaning of a problem... They analyze givens, constraints, relationships, and goals. They make conjectures about the form... of the solution and plan a solution pathway...

In your book

Verbal Models and the **Problem Solving Plan** help you translate the information in a problem into a model and then analyze your solution.

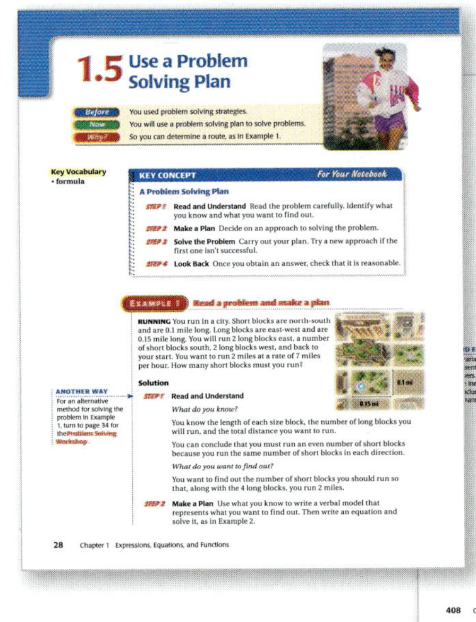

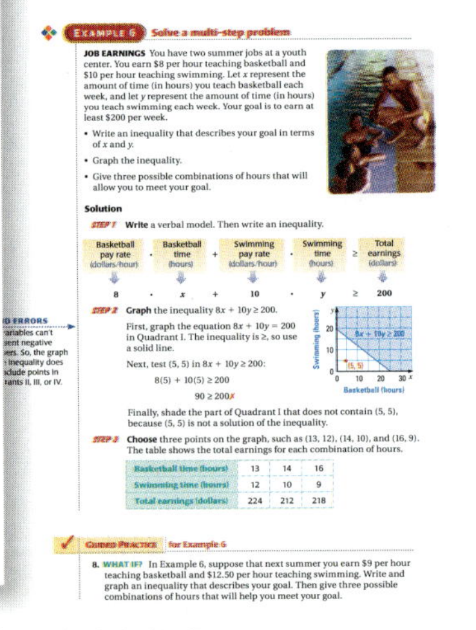

Rewrite Rational Expressions

GOAL Use division to rewrite rational expressions in different forms.

Rewriting a rational expression may reveal properties of the related function and its graph. For example, a simple rational function that can be rewritten in the *graphing form* $y = \dfrac{a}{x - h} + k$ reveals that it is a translation of the parent function $y = \dfrac{a}{x}$ with vertical asymptote $x = h$ and horizontal asymptote $y = k$.

EXAMPLE 1 **Rewrite and graph a rational function**

Rewrite the function $y = \dfrac{3x + 7}{x + 2}$ in graphing form. Then graph it.

Solution

Method 1

By inspection: $\dfrac{3x + 7}{x + 2} = \dfrac{3(x + 2) + 1}{x + 2} = 3 + \dfrac{1}{x + 2}$

Method 2

By long division:
$$\begin{array}{r} 3 \\ x + 2 \overline{)3x + 7} \\ \underline{3x + 6} \\ 1 \end{array}$$

The function in graphing form is $y = \dfrac{1}{x + 2} + 3$.

The graph is the graph of $y = \dfrac{1}{x}$ translated left 2 units and up 3 units.

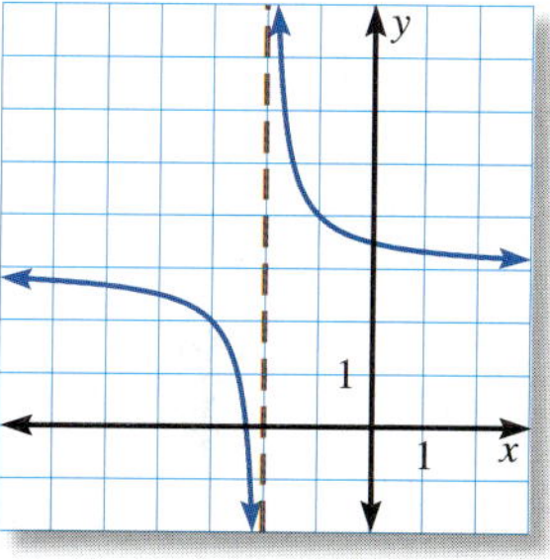

EXAMPLE 2 **Write an average cost function in graphing form**

GIFTS A company charges \$.20 each, plus a shipping charge of \$5.00, for a style of gift bag from its online store. Write an equation in graphing form for the average cost C per bag as a function of the number n of bags ordered. Then graph the function.

Solution

The average cost per bag is the total cost divided by the number of bags:

$$C = \frac{5 + 0.20n}{n} = \frac{5}{n} + \frac{0.20n}{n} = \frac{5}{n} + 0.2$$

The graph is that of $y = \dfrac{5}{n}$ translated up 0.2 unit. The cost cannot be negative, so graph only the portion in Quadrant I.

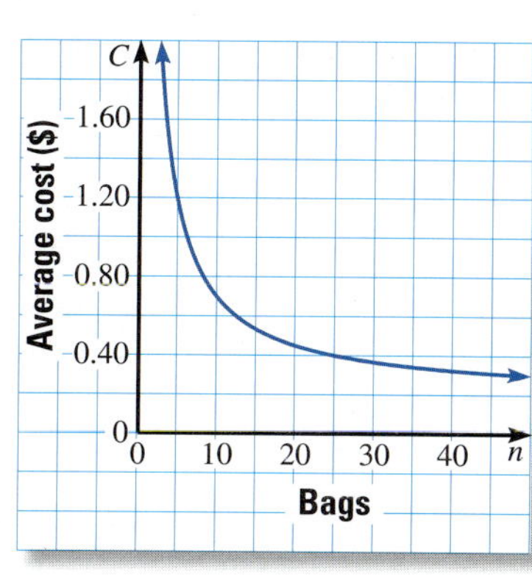

Write $\dfrac{2x^2 - x - 2}{x - 1}$ as the sum of a quotient and a remainder where the degree of the remainder's numerator is less than that of its denominator. What happens to the graph of the related function as $|x|$ increases without bound?

Solution

The divisor $x - 1$ is linear, so use synthetic division to evaluate when $x = 1$.

$$
\begin{array}{r|rrr}
1 & 2 & -1 & -2 \\
  &   & 2 & 1 \\
\hline
  & 2 & 1 & -1
\end{array}
\qquad
\dfrac{2x^2 - x - 2}{x - 1} = 2x + 1 + \dfrac{-1}{x - 1}
$$

Because the remainder term approaches 0 as $|x|$ increases without bound, the graph gets closer and closer to the graph of $y = 2x + 1$.

PRACTICE

EXAMPLES 1 AND 3 on pp. CC5–CC6 for Exs. 1–8

Rewrite each rational function in graphing form. Then graph it.

1. $y = \dfrac{2x - 4}{x - 3}$
2. $y = \dfrac{8x + 7}{2x + 1}$
3. $y = \dfrac{3x + 4}{x + 1}$
4. $y = \dfrac{5x + 1}{x - 2}$

Rewrite each rational function as the sum of a quotient and a remainder where the degree of the remainder's numerator is less than that of its denominator.

5. $y = \dfrac{3x^2 + 2x + 1}{x - 1}$
6. $y = \dfrac{x^2 + 3x + 2}{x^2 - 4}$
7. $y = \dfrac{2x^2 - 9}{x^2 + 2x + 1}$

8. **END BEHAVIOR** Write $\dfrac{x^4 + 2x^2 - 1}{x^2 + 2}$ as the sum of a quotient and a remainder where the degree of the remainder's numerator is less than that of its denominator. What happens to the graph of the related function as $|x|$ increases without bound? *Explain.*

EXAMPLE 2 on p. CC5 for Exs. 9–10

9. **T-SHIRTS** You are having T-shirts printed for a reunion. There is a set-up fee of \$35 and a charge of \$10 per shirt. Write an equation in graphing form that gives the average cost C per T-shirt as a function of the number n of T-shirts printed. Then graph the function.

10. **BATTING AVERAGE** A softball player's batting average is the ratio of hits to times at bat. So far this season, a player has 11 hits in 40 at-bats.

a. The player wants to know what her season batting average will be if she has a .350 batting average from her next at-bat through the remainder of the season. Write a rational expression for her season batting average where n is the number of at-bats remaining in the season.

b. Rewrite the expression in part (a) in graphing form. Can the player ever improve her batting average to .350 for the season? *Explain.*

c. The player gets a hit the next 10 at-bats in a row, then bats .400 for the remainder of the season. Write a new expression for her season batting average.

Investigate Polynomials, Rational Expressions, and Closure

GOAL Determine whether a set is closed under an operation.

If an operation is performed on members of a set and the result is always a member of that set, the set is *closed* under that operation. For example, the set {0, 1} is closed under multiplication because every possible product ($0 \cdot 0 = 0$, $0 \cdot 1 = 0$, and $1 \cdot 1 = 1$) is a member of the set. On the other hand, the set is not closed under addition because the sum $1 + 1 = 2$ is not a member of the set.

The table below lists several subsets of the set of real numbers and indicates whether they are closed under the four basic operations.

Set of numbers	Closed under addition?	Closed under subtraction?	Closed under multiplication?	Closed under division?
Whole numbers	Yes	No	Yes	No
Integers	Yes	Yes	Yes	No
Rational numbers	Yes	Yes	Yes	Yes
Real numbers	Yes	Yes	Yes	Yes

CLOSURE AND DIVISION
Exclude the undefined case of division by 0 when determining whether a set is closed under division.

Sets of algebraic expressions, like sets of numbers, can either be closed or not closed under an operation.

EXAMPLE 1 **Determine whether a set of polynomials is closed**

Tell whether the set of polynomials in a single variable with real coefficients is closed under (a) addition and (b) multiplication.

Recall that a polynomial is a monomial or a sum of monomials. Let two polynomials $p_1(x)$ and $p_2(x)$ have terms of the form $a_k x^k$ and $b_k x^k$, respectively, where the coefficients a_k and b_k are real numbers and k is a whole number.

a. Adding two polynomials involves adding like terms, so the sum $p_1(x) + p_2(x)$ has terms of the form $(a_k + b_k)x^k$. Since the set of real numbers is closed under addition, the coefficient $a_k + b_k$ is a real number. The exponent remains the whole number k. So, the sum $p_1(x) + p_2(x)$ is itself a polynomial, and the set of polynomials is closed under addition.

b. Multiplying two polynomials involves multiplying each term of one polynomial with each term of the other. Let $a_j x^j$ be a term of $p_1(x)$, and let $b_k x^k$ be a term of $p_2(x)$. Then the product $p_1(x) \cdot p_2(x)$ has terms of the form $a_j x^j \cdot b_k x^k = (a_j \cdot b_k)x^{j+k}$. Since the set of real numbers is closed under multiplication, the coefficient $a_j \cdot b_k$ is a real number. Since the set of whole numbers is closed under addition, the exponent $j + k$ is a whole number. So, the product $p_1(x) \cdot p_2(x)$ is itself a polynomial, and the set of polynomials is closed under multiplication.

Tell whether the set of rational expressions in a single variable with real coefficients is closed under (a) addition and (b) multiplication.

Recall that a rational expression is the quotient of two polynomials. Let $r_1(x) = \dfrac{p_1(x)}{p_2(x)}$ and $r_2(x) = \dfrac{p_3(x)}{p_4(x)}$ be two rational expressions with real coefficients where $p_2(x) \neq 0$ and $p_4(x) \neq 0$.

a. To add $r_1(x)$ and $r_2(x)$, you first must find a common denominator. You can use $p_2(x) \cdot p_4(x)$.

$$r_1(x) + r_2(x) = \frac{p_1(x)}{p_2(x)} + \frac{p_3(x)}{p_4(x)}$$

$$= \frac{p_1(x)}{p_2(x)}\left(\frac{p_4(x)}{p_4(x)}\right) + \frac{p_3(x)}{p_4(x)}\left(\frac{p_2(x)}{p_2(x)}\right)$$

$$= \frac{p_1(x) \cdot p_4(x) + p_3(x) \cdot p_2(x)}{p_2(x) \cdot p_4(x)}$$

Since the set of polynomials is closed under both addition and multiplication, both the numerator and denominator of the sum $r_1(x) + r_2(x)$ are polynomials. So, the sum $r_1(x) + r_2(x)$ is a rational expression, and the set of rational expressions is closed under addition.

b. Both the numerator and denominator of $r_1(x) \cdot r_2(x) = \dfrac{p_1(x) \cdot p_3(x)}{p_2(x) \cdot p_4(x)}$ are polynomials since the set of polynomials is closed under multiplication. So, the product $r_1(x) \cdot r_2(x)$ is a rational expression, and the set of rational expressions is closed under multiplication.

PRACTICE

1. Give an example showing that the set of integers is not closed under division.

EXAMPLE 1
on p. CC7
for Exs. 2–3

Determine whether the given set of algebraic expressions is closed under the given operation. *Explain.*

2. the set of polynomials in one variable with real coefficients; subtraction

3. the set of polynomials in one variable with real coefficients; division

EXAMPLE 2
on p. CC8
for Exs. 4–5

4. the set of rational expressions in one variable with real coefficients; subtraction

5. the set of rational expressions in one variable with real coefficients; division

Based on the operations under which the given set is closed, tell whether the set is most similar to *the set of whole numbers, the set of integers,* or *the set of rational numbers.*

6. the set of polynomials in one variable with real coefficients

7. the set of rational expressions in one variable with real coefficients

8.6A Describe and Compare Function Characteristics

Key Vocabulary
- **increasing**
- **decreasing**
- **odd function**
- **even function**

The graphs of $y = x$ and $y = 2^x$ rise from left to right for all real numbers. These functions are always **increasing**. The graphs of $y = -x$ and $y = 0.5^x$ fall from left to right for all real numbers. These functions are always **decreasing**. The function $y = x^2$ is decreasing for $x \le 0$, but increasing for $x \ge 0$. The table shows when a function is increasing or decreasing over an interval of its domain.

	Increasing over an interval	Decreasing over an interval
Values of $f(x)$	$f(x_1) < f(x_2)$ whenever $x_1 < x_2$.	$f(x_1) > f(x_2)$ whenever $x_1 < x_2$.
Graph of $f(x)$	Rises from left to right.	Falls from left to right.

EXAMPLE 1 Sketch a graph given a verbal description

FLYING Sketch a graph of $a(t)$ where a represents altitude and t represents time for the situation below. Label key information such as local minima and maxima and intervals where $a(t)$ is increasing or decreasing.

A small plane flying at a constant cruising altitude is caught in a storm. Air currents carry the plane up before pushing it down rapidly below its original altitude. The plane exits the storm and returns gradually to its cruising altitude.

Solution

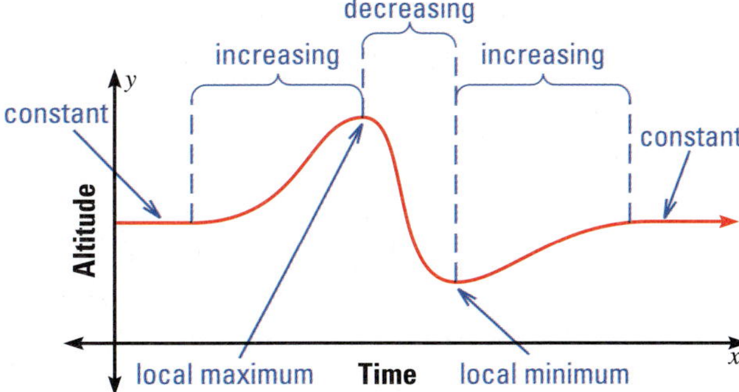

✓ **GUIDED PRACTICE** for Example 1

1. Sketch a graph for the situation described below. Label key information.

   The US gross domestic product (GDP) growth rate over a 2 year period can be modeled by a polynomial that began slightly positive before dropping to significantly negative, swinging back to significantly positive, then falling to a growth rate a little higher than at the beginning of the period.

AVERAGE RATE OF CHANGE For a *linear* function, the rate of change is *constant*, and is indicated by the slope. Even for a nonlinear function, however, you can find the *average* rate of change over any interval by finding the slope of the segment that connects the points on the graph determined by the endpoints of the interval.

The graph of $f(x) = \log_3 x$ at the right shows that $f(x)$ is always increasing. You can see, however, that the slope between the labeled pairs of points decreases as x increases, that is, the average rate of change is decreasing over successive x-intervals. So, although the graph is always rising, the rise becomes slower and slower for greater and greater x-values.

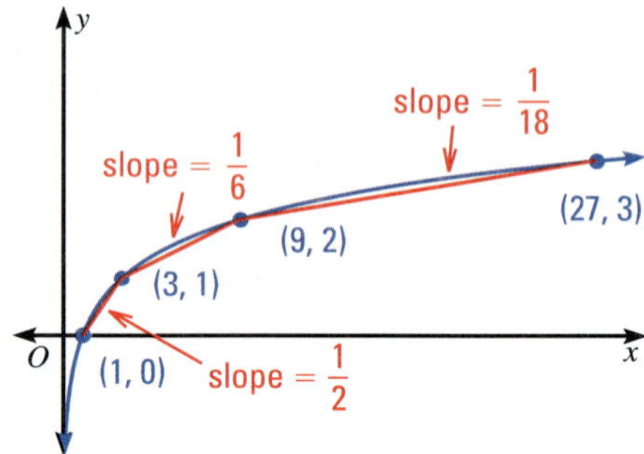

<hr>

EXAMPLE 2 **Investigate average rate of change**

For the function $f(x) = 2^{x-2} + 1$, find the average rate of change over the intervals $[-2, 0]$, $[0, 2]$, $[2, 4]$, $[4, 6]$, and $[6, 8]$. What happens to the average rate of change as x increases? What does this mean for the graph of $f(x)$?

Solution

The average rate of change over an interval $[x_1, x_2]$ is $\dfrac{f(x_2) - f(x_1)}{x_2 - x_1}$.

Interval	Average rate of change
$[-2, 0]$	$\dfrac{(2^{0-2} + 1) - (2^{-2-2} + 1)}{2} = \dfrac{1.25 - 1.0625}{2} = 0.09375$
$[0, 2]$	$\dfrac{(2^{2-2} + 1) - (2^{0-2} + 1)}{2} = \dfrac{2 - 1.25}{2} = 0.375$
$[2, 4]$	$\dfrac{(2^{4-2} + 1) - (2^{2-2} + 1)}{2} = \dfrac{5 - 2}{2} = 1.5$
$[4, 6]$	$\dfrac{(2^{6-2} + 1) - (2^{4-2} + 1)}{2} = \dfrac{17 - 5}{2} = 6$
$[6, 8]$	$\dfrac{(2^{8-2} + 1) - (2^{6-2} + 1)}{2} = \dfrac{65 - 17}{2} = 24$

The average rate of change is always positive, so the graph always rises. The average rate of change increases over successive intervals of the domain (by a factor of 4 for each increase of 2 in x). Because the average rate of change over each interval is equivalent to the slope of the segment from $(x_1, f(x_1))$ to $(x_2, f(x_2))$, the graph rises more and more steeply as x increases.

✓ **GUIDED PRACTICE** for Example 2

2. For the function $f(x) = -\log_2 x$, find the average rate of change over the intervals $[0.125, 0.25]$, $[0.25, 0.5]$, $[0.5, 1]$, $[1, 2]$, and $[2, 4]$. What does this mean for the graph?

 Compare functions in different representations

AREA AND VOLUME Anna and Zeke cut squares from the corners of rectangular pieces of cardboard and fold up the sides to make open boxes. Anna's cardboard is 10 inches by 12 inches. Zeke's is 8 inches by 15 inches. The volume V as a function of cut-out side length x is shown for Anna at the right and Zeke below.

Zeke's volume: $V(x) = x(8 - 2x)(15 - 2x)$

Compare the maximums and x-intercepts of the functions. Interpret the significance of the results.

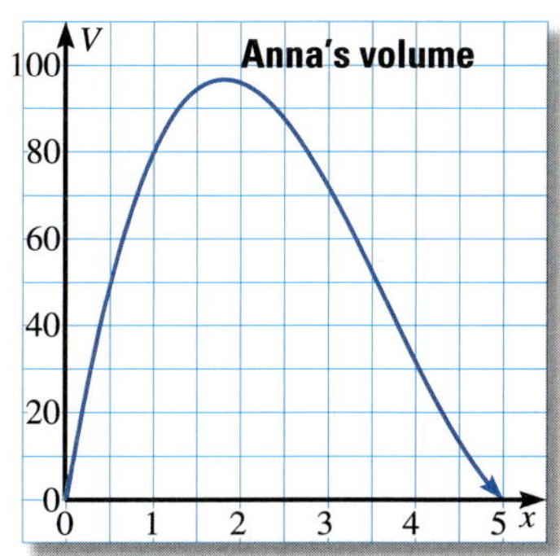

Solution

Use a graphing calculator for Zeke's function. The maximum is about 91 when x is about 1.7. The graph for Anna shows a maximum of about 97 when x is about 1.8. The pieces of cardboard have equal area, but Anna can make a box with greater volume.

The x-intercepts, which represent cut-out sizes that correspond to volumes of 0, are 0 and 4 for Zeke, and 0 and 5 for Anna. The volume of Anna's box decreases less with increasing cut-out size.

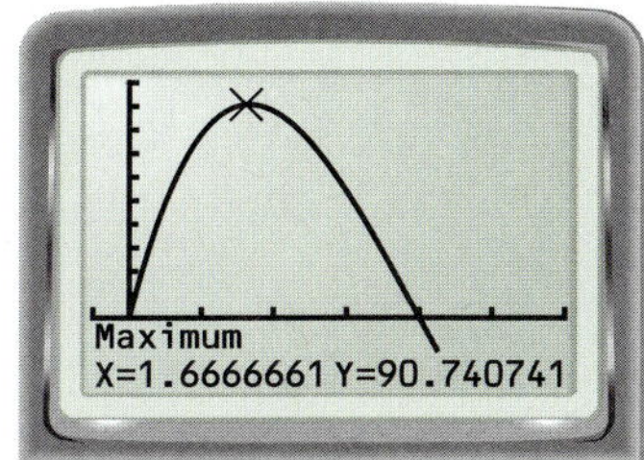

 Compare functions in different representations

FOOTBALL Fantasy football participants "draft" players for their teams. Below are models predicting fantasy points for two positions as a function of the player's rank. Compare fantasy points as a function of rank for the models.

INTERPRET THE TABLE

The table predicts the top tight end will score 175 fantasy points, but the 20th ranked tight end will score only 60 fantasy points.

Tight Ends

Rank	Fantasy points
1	175
10	90
20	60
30	45
40	35
50	25

Running Backs

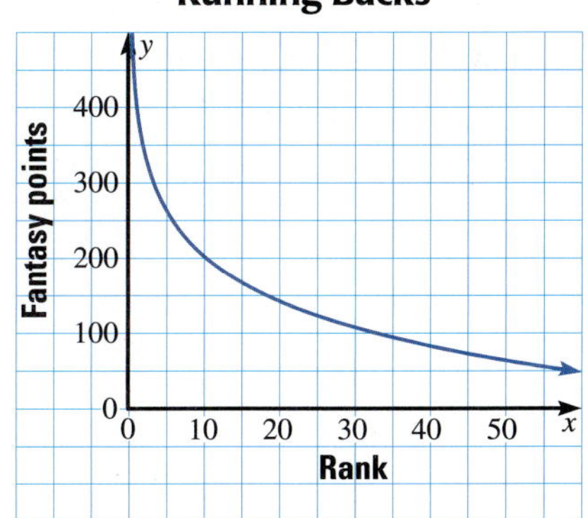

Solution

Use the graph to estimate the ordered pairs (rank, fantasy points) for running backs that correspond to the ordered pairs for tight ends from the table.

Tight ends: (1, 175)   (10, 90)   (20, 60)   (30, 45)   (40, 35)   (50, 25)

Running backs: (1, 400)   (10, 200)   (20, 140)   (30, 110)   (40, 85)   (50, 65)

Comparing ordered pairs, the points for running backs are always greater than for tight ends for each rank over the domain shown, but for running backs, the points decrease more rapidly as rank changes than for tight ends.

EVEN AND ODD FUNCTIONS A function f is an **even function** if $f(-x) = f(x)$ for all x in its domain. The graph of an even function is symmetric about the y-axis. A function f is an **odd function** if $f(-x) = -f(x)$ for all x in its domain. The graph of an odd function is *symmetric about the origin*. One way to recognize a graph that is symmetric about the origin is that it looks the same after a 180° rotation about the origin.

Even Function

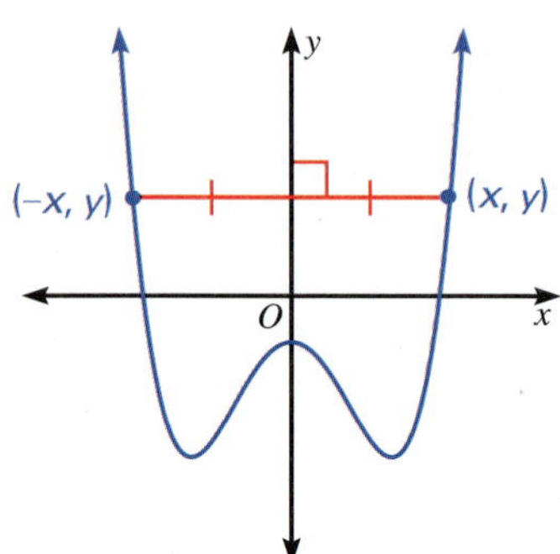

Odd Function

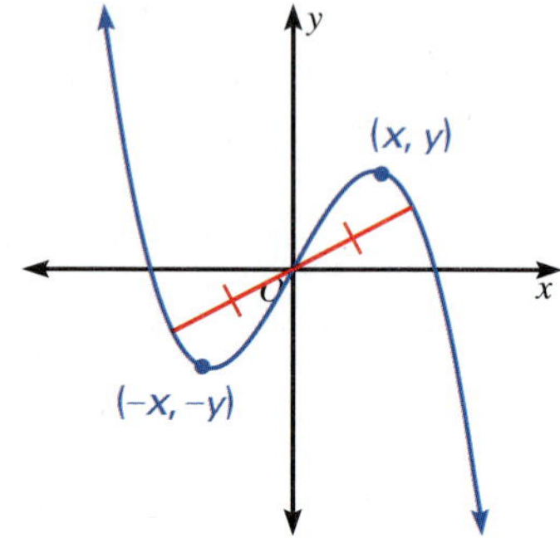

For an even function, if (x, y) is on the graph, then $(-x, y)$ is also on the graph. The y-axis is the perpendicular bisector of the segment between any pair of points (x, y) and $(-x, y)$.

For an odd function, if (x, y) is on the graph, then $(-x, -y)$ is also on the graph. The origin bisects the segment between any pair of points (x, y) and $(-x, -y)$.

EXAMPLE 5 **Identify even and odd functions**

Determine whether the function is *even*, *odd*, or *neither*.

a. $f(x) = x^3 - 7x$ **b.** $g(x) = \dfrac{6}{x + 1}$

Solution

a. Replace x with $-x$ in the equation for the function, and then simplify.

$$f(-x) = (-x)^3 - 7(-x) = -x^3 + 7x = -(x^3 - 7x) = -f(x)$$

Because $f(-x) = -f(x)$, the function is odd.

b. $g(-x) = \dfrac{6}{(-x) + 1} = \dfrac{6}{-x + 1}$

Because $\dfrac{6}{-x + 1} \neq \dfrac{6}{x + 1}$ and $\dfrac{6}{-x + 1} \neq -\dfrac{6}{x + 1}$, $g(x)$ is neither even nor odd.

✓ **GUIDED PRACTICE** **for Examples 3–5**

3. Refer to Example 4. For quarterbacks, the equation $y = 475 - 110 \ln x$ models fantasy points as a function of rank. Compare the point totals as a function of rank for quarterbacks and running backs.

4. Determine whether $f(x) = -x^6 + 3x^4 - 2x^2 - 7$ is *even*, *odd*, or *neither*.

5. Determine whether $f(x) = \dfrac{-5x}{12 - x^2 - x^4}$ is *even*, *odd*, or *neither*.

SKILL PRACTICE

EXAMPLE 1
on p. CC9
for Exs. 3–5

1. **VOCABULARY** Copy and complete: A function f is a(n) __?__ function if $f(-x) = f(x)$ for all values of x in the domain of f.

2. ★ **WRITING** *Describe* how to determine when a function is increasing or decreasing over its domain or over an interval of its domain.

SKETCHING GRAPHS **Sketch a graph for each situation. Label key information, including local extremes, intercepts, and intervals of increase or decrease.**

3. The number of customers $c(t)$ in a coffee shop t hours after it opens is as follows: opens with no customers, increases until midmorning, decreases, increases at lunch to its greatest number of customers for the day, then slowly decreases until the shop closes in the late afternoon.

4. Your height $h(t)$ in feet above the ground t seconds from the beginning of an amusement park ride is as follows: starts at its highest point, quickly drops halfway to the ground, climbs back up—but not as high as before—then quickly drops to the ground, leveling out at the end.

5. The normal fill level of a reservoir is marked as "0" on a marker pole. The water level $w(t)$ where t is in weeks drops slowly and steadily from the fill level during a summer drought, then rapidly rises well above fill level from large storms. The level is then brought back down to the fill level, where it is held constant.

EXAMPLE 2
on p. CC10
for Exs. 6–11

INVESTIGATING RATES OF CHANGE **Find the average rate of change of the function over the given intervals. Describe what happens to the graph of the function as x increases.**

6. $f(x) = 3^{x+4} - 6$ over the intervals $[-4, -3]$, $[-3, -2]$, $[-2, -1]$, $[-1, 0]$

7. $f(x) = \log_{1/2}(x - 3)$ over the intervals $[4, 5]$, $[5, 7]$, $[7, 11]$, $[11, 19]$

8.

x	−1	0	1	2	3
$f(x)$	−1	−0.5	0.25	1.375	3.0625

9.

x	$\frac{7}{3}$	3	5	11	29
$f(x)$	−1	0	1	2	3

10. **ERROR ANALYSIS** *Describe* and correct the error in the statement about the function graphed at the right.

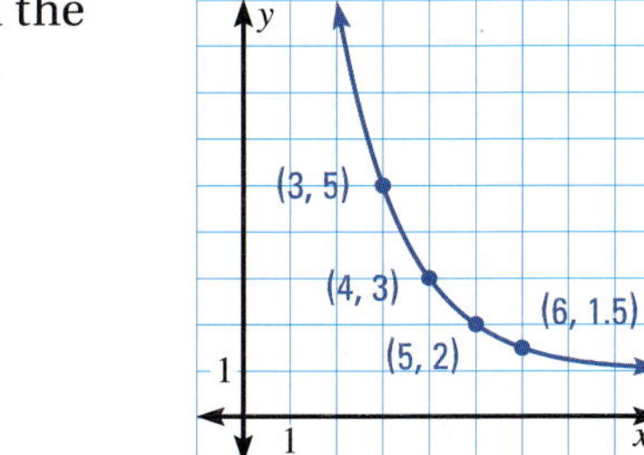

As x increases, the absolute value of the average rate of change of the function increases.

11. ★ **SHORT RESPONSE** You are given a function rule for a function $f(x)$ and an interval $[x_1, x_2]$ for which $x_2 > x_1$. You determine that $f(x_2) > f(x_1)$. Can you conclude that $f(x)$ is increasing over the interval $[x_1, x_2]$? *Explain.*

EXAMPLES 3 AND 4
on p. CC11
for Exs. 12–14

COMPARING FUNCTIONS Compare the properties of the two functions and the key characteristics of their graphs. Include information such as the domain and range, asymptotes, end behavior, and general appearance of the graphs.

12. **Function 1:** an inverse variation function with constant of variation $a = 25$

   Function 2: $y = -\dfrac{1}{x}$

13. **Function 1:** a square root function whose graph passes through the points $(0, 0)$, $(1, 1)$, $(4, 2)$, $(9, 3)$

   Function 2: $y = 3\sqrt{x - 1} + 5$

14. ★ **MULTIPLE CHOICE** Which statement is true about the functions shown?

   Function 1: $y = \log(x - 4)$ **Function 2:**

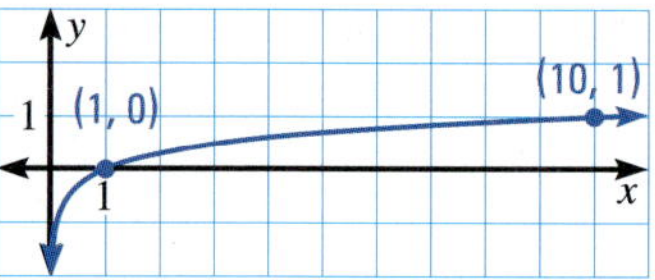

   Ⓐ The graphs of the functions have the same x-intercept.

   Ⓑ The functions have the same domain.

   Ⓒ The functions have the same asymptote(s).

   Ⓓ The functions have the same range.

EXAMPLE 5
on p. CC12
for Exs. 15–24

IDENTIFYING EVEN AND ODD FUNCTIONS Determine whether the function is *even*, *odd*, or *neither*.

15. 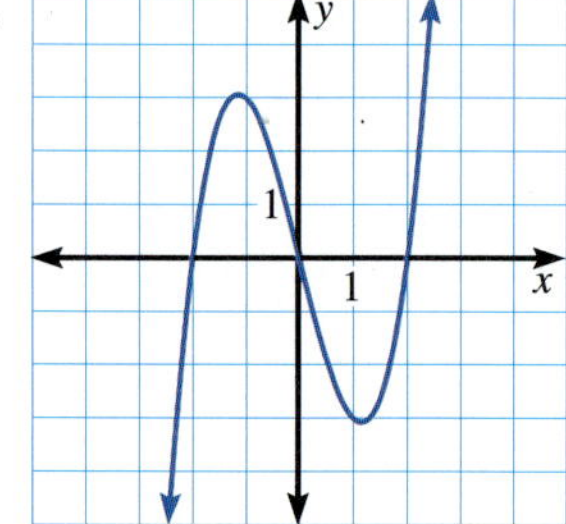   16. 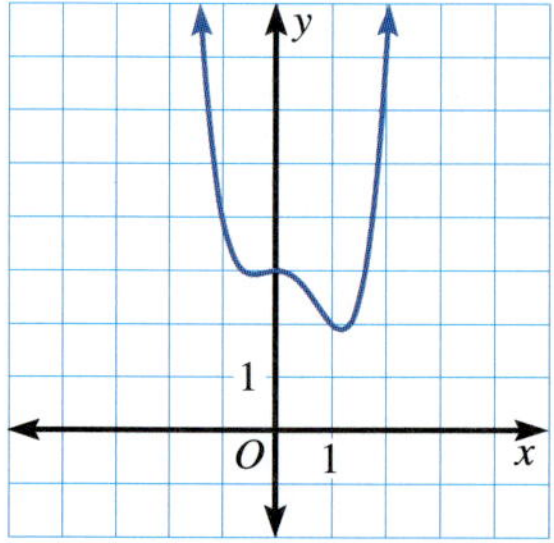   17. 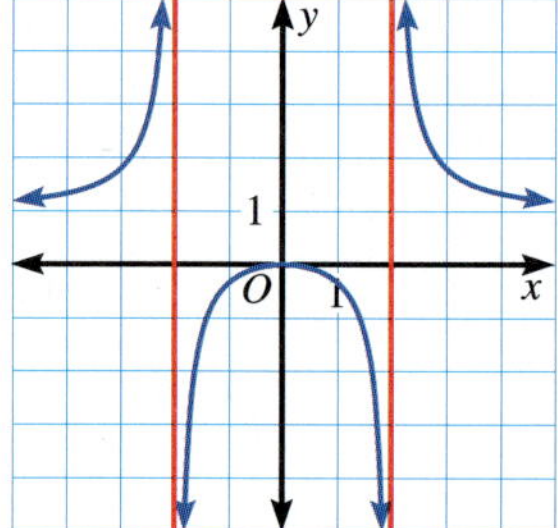

18. $f(x) = x^2 + x$ 19. $g(x) = x^5 + x^3 + x$ 20. $g(x) = x^4 + 2x^2$

21. $k(x) = 5x^6 + 9x^4 + x^2$ 22. $m(x) = \dfrac{12}{x}$ 23. $m(x) = \dfrac{3}{x} + 5$

24. ★ **MULTIPLE CHOICE** Which function is even?

   Ⓐ $g(x) = 11x^6 + 7x^2$ Ⓑ $k(x) = 8x^7 - x^5 + 12x^3$

   Ⓒ $h(x) = \dfrac{9}{x}$ Ⓓ $j(x) = \dfrac{11}{x + 2} - 4$

25. **CHALLENGE** Tell whether each statement is *always*, *sometimes*, or *never* true. *Explain.*

   a. The product of two even functions is an even function.

   b. The product of two odd functions is an odd function.

**EXAMPLES
3 AND 4**
on p. CC11
for Exs. 26–28

26. PACKAGING Box 1 and Box 2 are open boxes formed by cutting squares from the corners of rectangular pieces of cardboard and folding up the sides. The cardboard for Box 1 is 8 inches by 3 inches, and the cardboard for Box 2 is 6 inches by 4 inches. The volume V (in cubic inches) for Box 1 is $V = x(8 - 2x)(3 - 2x)$, where x is the side length of the square cut-outs. The volume for Box 2 is shown in the graph. Compare the x-intercepts and the maximums of the functions. Interpret the significance of the results.

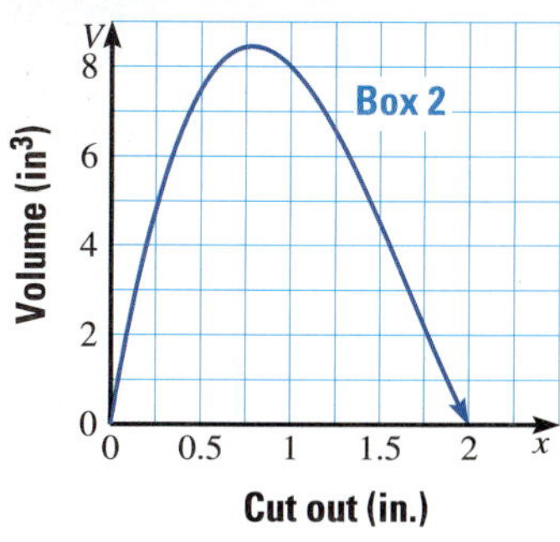

27. AUTOMOBILES The function $y = 25{,}000(0.82)^t$ gives the value y (in dollars) of one model of minivan as it depreciates over t years. The graph at the right shows the depreciating value of one model of sports utility vehicle. Compare y-intercepts and the rate of decrease in value for each vehicle. Interpret the significance of the results.

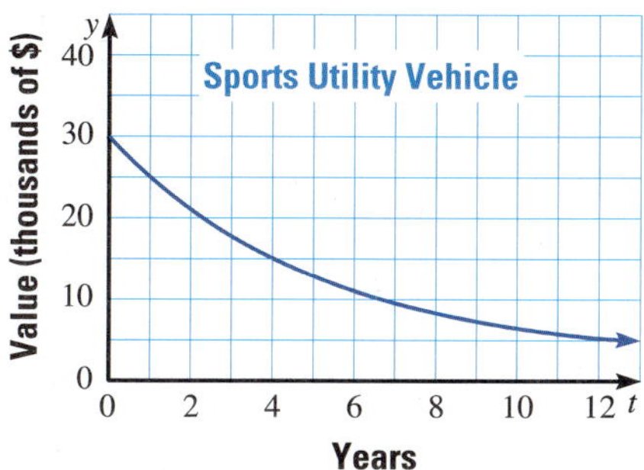

28. PACKAGING A company uses two 1200 cubic centimeter containers for powdered art supplies: a cylinder and a rectangular prism with a square base. The cylinder's diameter is the same as a side of the prism's base. The graph shows surface area S as a function of diameter d for the cylinder. The ordered pairs $(d, S(d))$ below are for the prism.

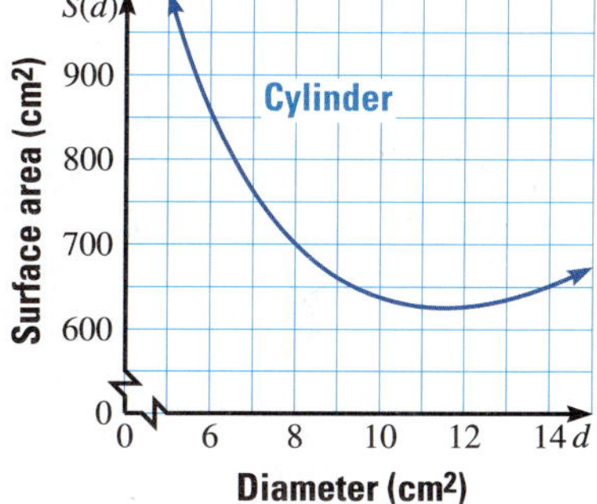

(9.4, 687.4), (9.8, 681.9), (10.2, 678.7),

(10.6, 677.6), (11, 678.4), (11.4, 681.0)

a. Compare the minimum surface areas and corresponding values of d.

b. The respective heights of the prism and cylinder are $h = \dfrac{1200}{d^2}$ and $h = \dfrac{4800}{\pi d^2}$. Compare the heights that correspond to the minimum surface areas for the containers. What do you notice?

29. FINANCE You and your sister deposit money in a savings account.

a. You deposit $1000 into an account that pays 2.8% annual interest, compounded annually. Copy and complete the table to determine the account balance A (rounded to the nearest cent) after t years.

t (years)	1	2	3	4	5
A (dollars)	?	?	?	?	?

b. The balance in your sister's account is given by $A = 1500(1.0175)^t$ after t years. Compare this function to the function in part (a). Interpret what your observations mean in the context of the situation.

30. ★ **OPEN-ENDED** Give a real-world example of a situation that can be modeled by a function that is decreasing, but for which the magnitude of the average rate of change is getting less and less.

31. ★ **EXTENDED RESPONSE** Observe the patterns below.

   Pattern 1: 1, 16, 81, 256, …

   Pattern 2: 4, 16, 64, 256, …

   a. **Model** Each pattern can be represented using ordered pairs (x, y), where x is the position of the number in the pattern and y is the number. For example, Pattern 1 can be represented as (1, 1), (2, 16), (3, 81), and so on. Write a function rule that models the ordered pairs for each pattern.

   b. **Graph** Graph both functions from part (a) on the same set of axes. Does the value of one function eventually exceed and increase more rapidly than the value of the other as x continues to increase? *Explain*.

   c. **Interpret** In general, as the value of x increases will a quantity that is increasing exponentially eventually exceed a quantity that is increasing as a polynomial function? *Explain* your reasoning and give examples to support your answer.

32. **CHALLENGE** A manufacturer produces an open box with two flaps from a square piece of cardboard by cutting congruent rectangles from each corner. The height of each of the rectangles is equal to twice its width.

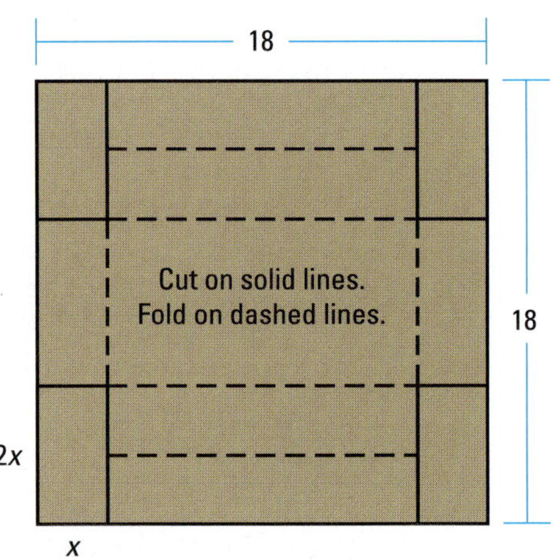

   a. A box like the one described above is made from an 18 inch square piece of cardboard. The volume V (in cubic inches) of the box is $V = x(18 - 2x)(18 - 4x)$. Find the average rate of change of the function over the intervals [0, 1], [1, 2], [2, 3], and [3, 4].

   b. Does a maximum or minimum value occur over any of the intervals in part (a)? If so, is it a maximum or a minimum? *Explain* your reasoning.

MIXED REVIEW

Write an equation of the line that passes through the given point and satisfies the given condition. *(Lesson 2.4)*

33. $(-6, 1)$; parallel to $y = 5x - 2$

34. $(3, -3)$; perpendicular to $y = -4x + 1$

PREVIEW
Prepare for Lesson 9.1 in Exs. 35–40.

Simplify the expression. *(Lesson 4.5)*

35. $\sqrt{27}$ 36. $\sqrt{32}$ 37. $\sqrt{150}$

38. $\sqrt{108}$ 39. $\sqrt{242}$ 40. $\sqrt{98}$

Simplify the expression. Assume all variables are positive. *(Lesson 6.2)*

41. $\dfrac{5\sqrt{x^3 y} - 3\sqrt{xy^5}}{\sqrt{xy}}$ 42. $\sqrt[3]{16x^4 y^2} \cdot \sqrt[3]{4x^2 yz}$ 43. $\dfrac{\sqrt[5]{xy} + 5\sqrt[5]{xy}}{2\sqrt[5]{x^6 y^7}}$

○ = **WORKED-OUT SOLUTIONS** for Exs. 5 and 27   ★ = **STANDARDIZED TEST PRACTICE**

10.5A Find Probabilities of Independent and Dependent Events

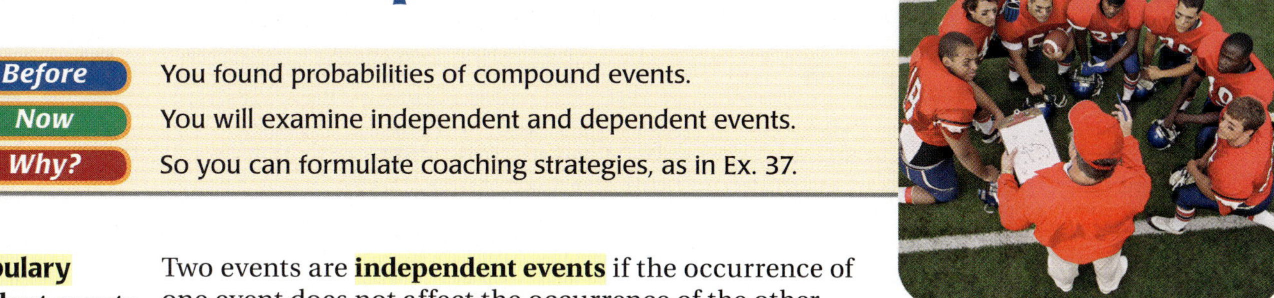

Before	You found probabilities of compound events.
Now	You will examine independent and dependent events.
Why?	So you can formulate coaching strategies, as in Ex. 37.

Key Vocabulary
• independent events
• dependent events
• conditional probability

Two events are **independent events** if the occurrence of one event does not affect the occurrence of the other. Two events are **dependent events** if the occurrence of one event *does* affect the occurrence of the other.

EXAMPLE 1 Identify independent and dependent events

A jar contains red and blue marbles. You randomly choose a marble from the jar, and you do not replace it. Then you randomly choose another marble. Tell whether the events are *independent* or *dependent*.

> **Event *A*:** The first marble you choose is red.
> **Event *B*:** The second marble you choose is blue.

Solution

After you choose a red marble, fewer marbles remain in the jar. This affects the probability that the second marble is blue. So, the events are dependent.

CONDITIONAL PROBABILITIES
The conditional probability of *B* given *A* can be greater than, less than, or equal to the probability of *B*.

The probability that event *B* occurs given that event *A* has occurred is called the **conditional probability** of *B* given *A* and is written $P(B|A)$. Note that *A* and *B* are independent events if and only if $P(B) = P(B|A)$ since the probability of event *B* does not depend on the occurrence of event *A*.

KEY CONCEPT *For Your Notebook*

Probabilities of Independent and Dependent Events

Independent Events

For two independent events *A* and *B*, the probability that both events occur is the product of the probabilities of the events.

$$P(A \text{ and } B) = P(A) \cdot P(B) \qquad \textit{Events A and B are independent.}$$

Dependent Events

For two dependent events *A* and *B*, the probability that both occur is the product of the probability of the first event and the conditional probability of the second event given the first event.

$$P(A \text{ and } B) = P(A) \cdot P(B|A) \qquad \textit{Events A and B are dependent.}$$

The formulas for finding the probabilities of independent and dependent events can be extended to three or more events.

As part of a board game, you need to spin the spinner at the right, which is divided into equal parts. Find the probability that you get 25 on your first spin and 50 on your second spin.

Solution

Let event A be "get 25 on first spin" and let event B be "get 50 on second spin." Find the probability of each event. Then multiply the probabilities.

$$P(A) = \frac{2}{8} \qquad \text{"25" appears twice.}$$

$$P(B) = \frac{1}{8} \qquad \text{"50" appears once.}$$

$$P(A \text{ and } B) = P(A) \cdot P(B) = \frac{2}{8} \cdot \frac{1}{8} = \frac{2}{64} \approx 0.031$$

▶ The probability that you get 25 on your first spin and 50 on your second spin is about 3.1%.

A bowl contains 36 green grapes and 14 purple grapes. You randomly choose a grape, eat it, and randomly choose another grape. Find the probability that both events A and B will occur.

Event A: The first grape is green.
Event B: The second grape is green.

Solution

Find $P(A)$ and $P(B|A)$. Then multiply the probabilities.

$$P(A) = \frac{36}{50} \qquad \text{Of the 50 grapes, 36 are green.}$$

$$P(B|A) = \frac{35}{49} \qquad \text{Of the 49 remaining grapes, 35 are green.}$$

$$P(A \text{ and } B) = P(A) \cdot P(B|A) = \frac{36}{50} \cdot \frac{35}{49} = \frac{1260}{2450} \approx 0.514$$

▶ The probability that both of the grapes are green is about 51.4%.

✓ **GUIDED PRACTICE**   for Examples 1, 2, and 3

Tell whether the situation describes *independent* or *dependent* events. Then answer the question.

1. **CLOTHING** A drawer contains 12 white socks and 8 black socks. You randomly choose one sock, and you do not replace it. Then you randomly choose another sock. What is the probability that both socks chosen are white?

2. **COIN FLIPS** Suppose you flip a coin twice. What is the probability that you get tails on the first flip and tails on the second flip?

CONDITIONAL PROBABILITY You can rewrite the formula for dependent events from the first page of this lesson to give a rule for finding conditional probabilities. Dividing both sides of the formula by $P(A)$ gives the following.

$$P(B|A) = \frac{P(A \text{ and } B)}{P(A)}$$

EXAMPLE 4   Find a conditional probability

WEATHER The table shows the numbers of tropical cyclones that formed during the hurricane seasons from 1988 to 2004. Use the table to estimate **(a)** the probability that a future tropical cyclone in the Northern Hemisphere is a hurricane, and **(b)** the probability that a hurricane is in the Northern Hemisphere.

Type of Tropical Cyclone	Northern Hemisphere	Southern Hemisphere
Tropical depression	199	18
Tropical storm	398	200
Hurricane	545	215

Solution

a. $P(\text{hurricane}|\text{Northern Hemisphere})$

$= \dfrac{\text{Number of hurricanes in Northern Hemisphere}}{\text{Total number of cyclones in Northern Hemisphere}} = \dfrac{545}{1142} \approx 0.477$

b. $P(\text{Northern Hemisphere}|\text{hurricane})$

$= \dfrac{\text{Number of hurricanes in Northern Hemisphere}}{\text{Total number of hurricanes}} = \dfrac{545}{760} \approx 0.717$

EXAMPLE 5   Compare independent and dependent events

SELECTING CARDS You randomly select two cards from a standard deck of 52 cards. What is the probability that the first card is not a heart and the second is a heart if **(a)** you replace the first card before selecting the second, and **(b)** you do not replace the first card?

Solution

Let A be "the first card is not a heart" and B be "the second card is a heart."

AVOID ERRORS
It is important first to determine whether A and B are independent or dependent in order to calculate $P(A \text{ and } B)$ correctly.

a. If you replace the first card before selecting the second card, then A and B are independent events. So, the probability is:

$$P(A \text{ and } B) = P(A) \cdot P(B) = \frac{39}{52} \cdot \frac{13}{52} = \frac{3}{16} \approx 0.188$$

b. If you do not replace the first card before selecting the second card, then A and B are dependent events. So, the probability is:

$$P(A \text{ and } B) = P(A) \cdot P(B|A) = \frac{39}{52} \cdot \frac{13}{51} = \frac{13}{68} \approx 0.191$$

3. WHAT IF? Use the information in Example 4 to find **(a)** the probability that a future tropical cyclone is a tropical storm and **(b)** the probability that a future tropical cyclone in the Southern Hemisphere is a tropical storm.

Find the probability of drawing the given cards from a standard deck of 52 cards (a) with replacement and (b) without replacement.

4. A spade, then a club

5. A jack, then another jack

EXAMPLE 6   **Solve a multi-step problem**

SAFETY Using observations made of drivers arriving at a certain high school, a study reports that 69% of adults wear seat belts while driving. A high school student also in the car wears a seat belt 66% of the time when the adult wears a seat belt, and 26% of the time when the adult does not wear a seat belt. What is the probability that a high school student in the study wears a seat belt?

Solution

A probability tree diagram, where the probabilities are given along the branches, can help you solve the problem. Notice that the probabilities for all branches from the same point must sum to 1.

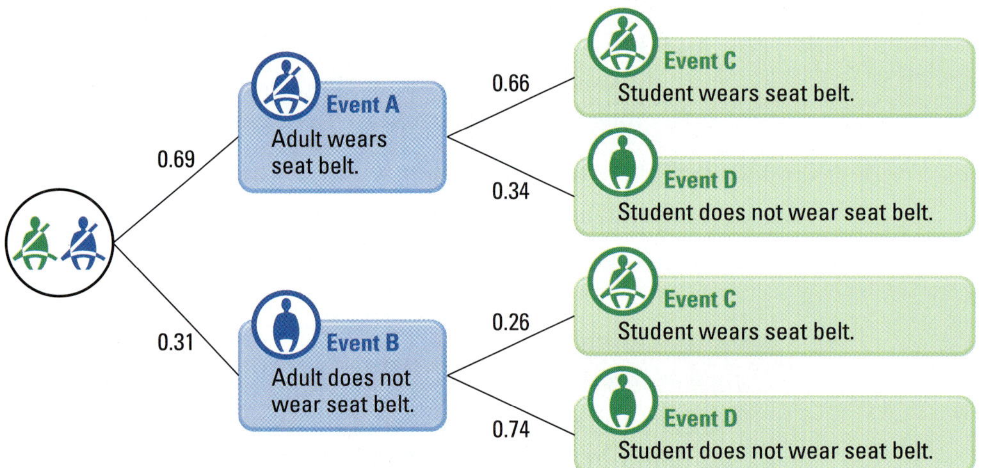

So, the probability that a high school student wears a seat belt is:

$$P(C) = P(A \text{ and } C) + P(B \text{ and } C)$$

$$= P(A) \cdot P(C|A) + P(B) \cdot P(C|B)$$

$$= (0.69)(0.66) + (0.31)(0.26) = 0.536$$

 **GUIDED PRACTICE**   for Example 6

6. BASKETBALL A high school basketball team leads at halftime in 60% of the games in a season. The team wins 80% of the time when they have the halftime lead, but only 10% of the time when they do not. What is the probability that the team wins a particular game during the season?

10.5A EXERCISES

SKILL PRACTICE

1. VOCABULARY Copy and complete: The probability that B will occur given that A has occurred is called the ___?___ of B given A.

2. ★ WRITING *Explain* the difference between dependent events and independent events, and give an example of each.

EXAMPLE 1
on p. CC17
for Exs. 3–6

INDEPENDENT AND DEPENDENT EVENTS Tell whether the events are *independent* or *dependent*.

3. A box of energy bars contains an assortment of flavors. You randomly choose an energy bar and eat it. Then you randomly choose another bar.

Event A:	You choose a honey-peanut bar first.
Event B:	You choose a chocolate chip bar second.

4. You roll a number cube and flip a coin.

Event A:	You get a 4 when rolling the number cube.
Event B:	You get tails when flipping the coin.

5. Your CD collection contains hip-hop and rock CDs. You randomly choose a CD, then choose another without replacing the first CD.

Event A:	You choose a hip-hop CD first.
Event B:	You choose a rock CD second.

6. There are 22 volumes of an encyclopedia on a shelf. You randomly choose a volume and put it back. Then you randomly choose another volume.

Event A:	You choose volume 7 first.
Event B:	You choose volume 5 second.

EXAMPLE 2
on p. CC18
for Exs. 7–11

INDEPENDENT EVENTS Events A and B are independent. Find the missing probability.

7. $P(A) = 0.7$
$P(B) = 0.3$
$P(A \text{ and } B) = $ ___?___

8. $P(A) = 0.22$
$P(B) = $ ___?___
$P(A \text{ and } B) = 0.11$

9. $P(A) = $ ___?___
$P(B) = 0.4$
$P(A \text{ and } B) = 0.13$

10. ★ MULTIPLE CHOICE Events A and B are independent. What is $P(A \text{ and } B)$ if $P(A) = 0.3$ and $P(B) = 0.2$?

(A) 0.06 **(B)** 0.1 **(C)** 0.5 **(D)** 0.6

11. REASONING Let $P(A) = 0.3$, $P(B) = 0.2$, and $P(A \text{ and } B) = 0.06$. Find $P(A|B)$ and $P(B|A)$. Tell if A and B are dependent or independent. *Explain.*

EXAMPLE 3
on p. CC18
for Exs. 12–14

DEPENDENT EVENTS Events A and B are dependent. Find the missing probability.

12. $P(A) = 0.5$
$P(B|A) = 0.4$
$P(A \text{ and } B) = $ ___?___

13. $P(A) = 0.9$
$P(B|A) = $ ___?___
$P(A \text{ and } B) = 0.72$

14. $P(A) = $ ___?___
$P(B|A) = 0.6$
$P(A \text{ and } B) = 0.15$

EXAMPLE 4
on p. CC19
for Exs. 15–18

CONDITIONAL PROBABILITY Let n be a randomly selected integer from 1 to 20. Find the indicated probability.

15. n is 2 given that it is even

16. n is 5 given that it is less than 8

17. n is prime given that it has 2 digits

18. n is odd given that it is prime

EXAMPLE 5
on p. CC19
for Exs. 19–26

DRAWING CARDS Find the probability of drawing the given cards from a standard deck of 52 cards **(a)** with replacement and **(b)** without replacement.

19. A club, then a spade

20. A queen, then an ace

21. A face card, then a 6

22. A 10, then a 2

23. A king, then a queen, then a jack

24. A spade, then a club, then another spade

25. **REASONING** You are playing a game that involves spinning the wheel shown. Find **(a)** the probability of spinning blue and **(b)** the probability of first spinning green and then spinning blue. Are the events of spinning green and then blue dependent or independent? *Explain.*

26. ★ **MULTIPLE CHOICE** What is the approximate probability of drawing 3 consecutive hearts from a standard deck of 52 cards without replacement?

  A 0.0122   **B** 0.0129   **C** 0.0156   **D** 0.0166

27. **ERROR ANALYSIS** Events A and B are independent. *Describe* and correct the error in finding $P(A \text{ and } B)$.

$$P(A) = 0.4, P(B) = 0.5$$
$$P(A \text{ and } B) = 0.4 + 0.5 = 0.9$$

28. ★ **OPEN-ENDED MATH** Flip a set of 3 coins and record the number of coins that come up heads. Repeat until you have a total of 10 trials.

  a. What is the experimental probability that a trial results in 2 heads?

  b. *Compare* your answer from part (a) with the theoretical probability that a trial results in 2 heads.

29. ★ **SHORT RESPONSE** A basket contains bottles of apple juice and orange juice in two sizes. The number of each type of bottle is shown in the table.

  a. What is the probability that a randomly chosen bottle of juice is a 6-ounce bottle given that the bottle contains apple juice?

  b. What is the probability that a randomly chosen 6-ounce bottle contains orange juice?

	6 oz	8 oz
Apple	4	8
Orange	6	9

  c. What is the probability that a randomly chosen bottle of orange juice is a 6-ounce bottle?

  d. Explain the difference between parts (b) and (c).

30. **REASONING** Let A and B be independent events. What is the relationship between $P(B)$ and $P(B|A)$? *Explain.*

◯ = **WORKED-OUT SOLUTIONS**
for Exs. 18 and 35

★ = **STANDARDIZED TEST PRACTICE**

31. CHALLENGE Bayes's Theorem states that $P(A|B) = \dfrac{P(B|A) \cdot P(A)}{P(B)}$. Prove it by using the formula for the probability of dependent events and another version of it in which A and B are swapped.

PROBLEM SOLVING

EXAMPLE 4
on p. CC19
for Exs. 32–34

32. ENVIRONMENT The table shows the numbers of species in the United States listed as endangered or threatened a few years ago. Find **(a)** the probability that a listed animal is a bird, **(b)** the probability that an endangered animal is a bird, and **(c)** the probability that a bird on the list is endangered.

	Endangered	Threatened
Mammals	69	9
Birds	77	14
Reptiles	14	22
Amphibians	11	10
Other	219	74

In Exercises 33 and 34, use the following information.

TRANSPORTATION All the students at Allen High School were surveyed to find out how they get to school each day. The table shows the number of students at each grade level who walk, bike, or take the bus to school.

	Walk	Bike	Bus	Total
Freshman	52	16	72	140
Sophomore	41	18	61	120
Junior	43	35	72	150
Senior	28	40	52	120
Total	164	109	257	530

33. a. What is the probability that a randomly chosen student is a senior?

    b. What is the probability that a randomly chosen student is a senior given that the student bikes to school?

    c. Are the events "student is a senior" and "student bikes to school" independent events? Why or why not?

34. a. What is the probability that a randomly chosen student takes the bus given that the student is a junior?

    b. What is the probability that a randomly chosen student who takes the bus is a junior?

    c. ★ **WRITING** Discuss the difference between the probabilities in parts (a) and (b).

EXAMPLE 6
on p. CC20
for Ex. 35

35. TENNIS A tennis player wins a match 55% of the time when she serves first and 47% of the time when her opponent serves first. The player who serves first is determined by a coin toss before the match. What is the probability that the player wins a given match?

EXAMPLE 6

on p. CC20
for Exs. 36–37

36. MEDICAL TESTING Suppose 1% of the population is known to have a medical condition. There is a test for the condition, and 80% of people with the condition test positive for it. Also, 10% of people without the condition test positive for it. Follow these steps to find the probability that a person actually has the condition given that he or she tests positive.

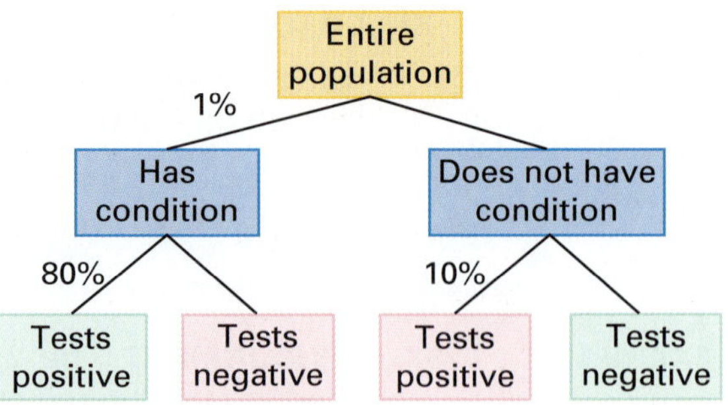

a. Let A be the event that a person has the condition and let B be the event that the person tests positive. What are $P(B|A)$ and $P(A)$?

b. Find $P(B)$. (*Hint:* Consider the portion of the population with the condition that tests positive and the portion of the population without the condition that tests positive.)

c. Use parts (a) and (b) and Bayes's Theorem to find the probability that a person has the condition given that he or she tests positive.

$$\textbf{Bayes's Theorem:} \quad P(A|B) = \frac{P(B|A) \cdot P(A)}{P(B)}$$

37. ★ EXTENDED RESPONSE A football team is losing by 14 points near the end of a game. The team scores two touchdowns (worth 6 points each) before the end of the game. After each touchdown, the coach must decide whether to go for 1 point with a kick (which is successful 99% of the time) or 2 points with a run or pass (which is successful 45% of the time).

a. Calculate If the team goes for 1 point after each touchdown, what is the probability that the coach's team wins? loses? ties?

b. Calculate If the team goes for 2 points after each touchdown, what is the probability that the coach's team wins? loses? ties?

c. Reasoning Can you develop a strategy so that the coach's team has a probability of winning the game that is greater than the probability of losing? If so, explain your strategy and calculate the probabilities of winning and losing using your strategy.

MIXED REVIEW

Simplify the expression. *(Lesson 5.3)*

38. $(x + 1)^2$

39. $(2a - 5)(3a + 4)$

40. $(b - 3)^3$

Let $f(x) = x^2 + 2$ and $g(x) = x - 4$. Perform the indicated operation and state the domain. *(Lesson 6.2)*

41. $f(x) + g(x)$

42. $f(x) - g(x)$

43. $f(x) \cdot g(x)$

44. $\dfrac{f(x)}{g(x)}$

45. $f(g(x))$

46. $g(f(x))$

47. $f(f(x))$

48. $g(g(x))$

Solve the equation.

49. $4^{x+1} = 8^{3x}$ *(Lesson 7.6)*

50. $4 \ln x = 10$ *(Lesson 7.6)*

51. $\dfrac{2}{x - 3} - \dfrac{1}{x + 2} = \dfrac{x - 5}{x + 2}$ *(Lesson 8.6)*

52. $\dfrac{x}{x - 2} + \dfrac{1}{x + 1} = \dfrac{2x + 1}{x + 1}$ *(Lesson 8.6)*

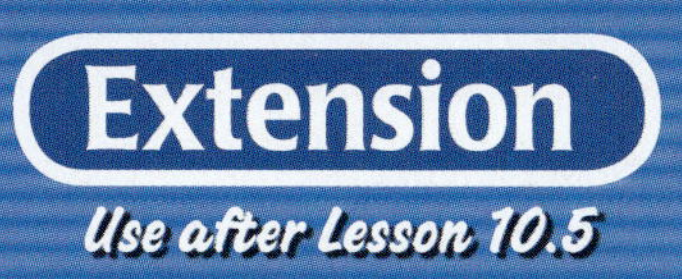

Make and Analyze Decisions

GOAL Use probabilities to make fair decisions and to analyze decisions and strategies.

Probabilities can help in making fair decisions, as when using a process with equally likely outcomes to select a contest winner. Probabilities also underlie all kinds of real-world decisions in business, science, agriculture, and so on.

EXAMPLE 1   Use probability to make a decision

Twenty students, including Noe, volunteer to present the "Best Teacher" award at a school banquet. Describe a process that gives Noe a fair chance to be chosen, and find the probability, if (a) "fair" means equally likely, and (b) "fair" means proportional to how many banquet prep hours the volunteer worked. Each volunteer worked at least one hour, Noe worked four hours, and, in all, the 20 students worked 45 hours.

Solution

a. Write the names on slips of paper, place them in a box, and draw a slip at random. The probability is 1 out of 20, or 5%.

b. Write the names on slips of paper, but for each hour more than one that a student worked, write their name on an extra slip. Then draw as in part (a). The probability is 4 out of 45, or about 8.9%.

EXAMPLE 2   Use probability to make a decision

Your company must produce 50,000 non-defective cell phones using a component from one of the suppliers below.

	Price per 1000	P(defective)	P(working)
Supplier X	$740.00	4.0%	96.0%
Supplier Y	$800.00	1.9%	98.1%

Each defective component bought results in $2.20 in extra cost to your company. From which supplier should you buy?

Solution

Use the probability that a component is defective to estimate the total cost.

$$\text{Total cost} = \frac{\text{Cost to get 50,000}}{\text{working components}} + \frac{\text{Extra cost from}}{\text{defective components}}$$

X: Solving $0.96x = 50{,}000$ gives $x = 52{,}083$. You must buy 53,000 components.
Total cost = $53{,}000(\$.74) + (0.04)(53{,}000)(\$2.20) = \$39{,}220 + \$4664 = \$43{,}884$

Y: Solving $0.981y = 50{,}000$ gives $y = 50{,}968$. You must buy 51,000 components.
Total cost = $51{,}000(\$.80) + (0.019)(51{,}000)(\$2.20) = \$40{,}800 + \$2132 = \$42{,}932$

▶ For the lowest total cost, you should buy from supplier Y.

EXAMPLE 1
on p. CC25
for Ex. 1

1. A teacher tells students, "For each puzzler you complete, I will assign you a prize entry." In all, 10 students complete 53 puzzlers. Leon completed 7. To award the prize, the teacher sets a calculator to generate a random integer from 1 to 53. Leon is assigned 18 to 24 as "winners." Is this fair to Leon according to the original instructions? *Explain.*

EXAMPLE 2
on p. CC25
for Exs. 2–4

2. A company creates a new brand of a snack, N, and tests it against the current market leader, L. The table shows the results.

	Prefer L	Prefer N
Current L consumer	72	46
Not current L consumer	52	114

Use probability to explain how the company's decisions about whether to try to improve the snack before marketing it and to which consumers it should aim its marketing might differ if the total size of the snack's market is expected to (a) change very little, and (b) expand very rapidly.

3. The Redbirds trail the Bluebirds by 1 goal with 1 minute left in the hockey game. The coach must decide whether to remove the goalie and add a frontline player. The only way the Redbirds can tie the game is for them to score and for the Bluebirds not to score. The probabilities are shown below.

	Goalie	No Goalie
Redbirds score	0.1	0.3
Bluebirds score	0.1	0.6

a. Find the probability that the Redbirds score and the Bluebirds do not score if the coach leaves the goalie in.

b. Find the probability that the Redbirds score and the Bluebirds do not score if the coach takes the goalie out.

c. Based on parts (a) and (b), what should the coach do?

4. A farmer is offered a contract that guarantees him $11.00 per bushel for his entire soybean crop when it is harvested in three months. Below are predictions for the market price m per of soybeans in three months.

$$P(m \le \$9.00) = 10\% \qquad P(m \ge \$10.50) = 50\%$$
$$P(m \ge \$12.50) = 20\%$$

The farmer predicts a total crop of 20,000 bushels, with a 30% chance of less than 15,000 bushels, and a 20% chance of at least 25,000 bushels.

a. Find the probability and income range for (i) the best case: the farmer declines the contract, the price is highest, and the harvest is largest; and (ii) the worst case: he declines the contract, the price is lowest, and the harvest is smallest. (Assume harvest size and price are independent.)

b. How much will the farmer make if he accepts the contract and his total crop prediction is accurate? How might this and the answers to part (a) affect the decision of whether or not to accept the contract?

Mastering the Standards

for Mathematical Practice

The topics described in the Standards for Mathematical Content will vary from year to year. However, the *way* in which you learn, study, and think about mathematics will not. The Standards for Mathematical Practice describe skills that you will use in all of your math courses.

Mathematical Practices

1. *Make sense of problems and persevere in solving them.*
2. *Reason abstractly and quantitatively.*
3. *Construct viable arguments and critique the reasoning of others.*
4. *Model with mathematics.*
5. *Use appropriate tools strategically.*
6. *Attend to precision.*
7. *Look for and make use of structure.*
8. *Look for and express regularity in repeated reasoning.*

4 Model with mathematics.

Mathematically proficient students can apply... mathematics... to... problems... in everyday life, society, and the workplace...

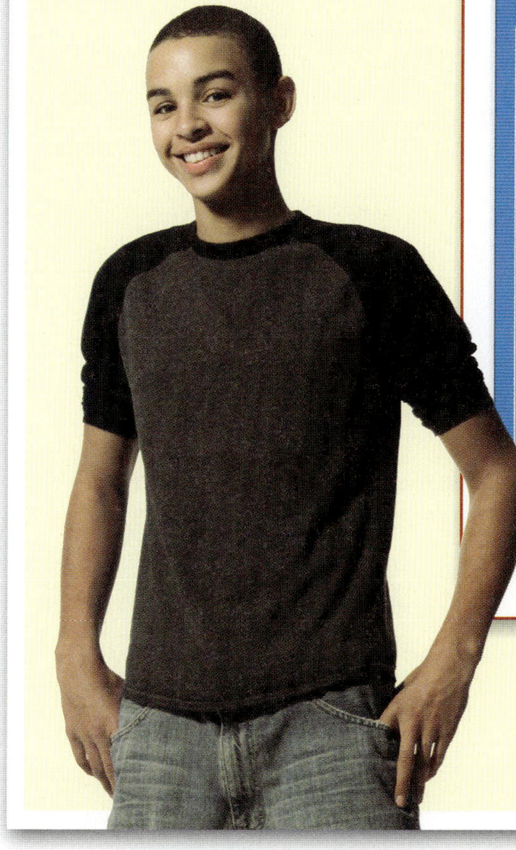

PhotoDisc/Getty Images

In your book

Application exercises and **Mixed Reviews of Problem Solving** apply mathematics to other disciplines and in real-world scenarios.

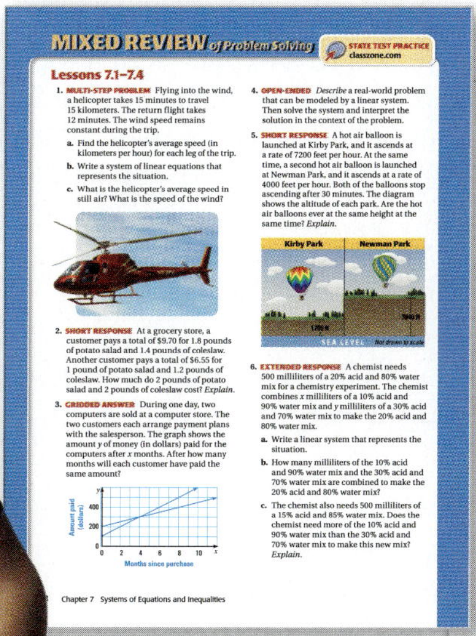

MIXED REVIEW of Problem Solving

STATE TEST PRACTICE classzone.com

Lessons 7.1–7.4

1. MULTI-STEP PROBLEM Flying into the wind, a helicopter takes 15 minutes to travel 15 kilometers. The return flight takes 12 minutes. The wind speed remains constant during the trip.
   a. Find the helicopter's average speed (in kilometers per hour) for each leg of the trip.
   b. Write a system of linear equations that represents the situation.
   c. What is the helicopter's average speed in still air? What is the speed of the wind?
2. SHORT RESPONSE At a grocery store, a customer pays a total of $9.70 for 1.8 pounds of potato salad and 1.4 pounds of coleslaw. Another customer pays a total of $6.55 for 1 pound of potato salad and 1.2 pounds of coleslaw. How much do 2 pounds of potato salad and 2 pounds of coleslaw cost? *Explain.*
3. GRIDDED ANSWER During one day, two computers are sold at a computer store. The two customers each arrange payment plans with the salesperson. The graph shows the amount y of money (in dollars) paid for the computers after x months. After how many months will each customer have paid the same amount?

4. OPEN-ENDED *Describe* a real-world problem that can be modeled by a linear system. Then solve the system and interpret the solution in the context of the problem.
5. SHORT RESPONSE A hot air balloon is launched at Kirby Park, and it ascends at a rate of 7200 feet per hour. At the same time, a second hot air balloon is launched at Newman Park, and it ascends at a rate of 4000 feet per hour. Both of the balloons stop ascending after 30 minutes. The diagram shows the altitude of each park. Are the hot air balloons ever at the same height at the same time? *Explain.*

6. EXTENDED RESPONSE A chemist needs 500 milliliters of a 20% acid and 80% water mix for a chemistry experiment. The chemist combines x milliliters of a 10% acid and 90% water mix and y milliliters of a 30% acid and 70% water mix to make the 20% acid and 80% water mix.
   a. Write a linear system that represents the situation.
   b. How many milliliters of the 10% acid and 90% water mix and the 30% acid and 70% water mix are combined to make the 20% acid and 80% water mix?
   c. The chemist also needs 500 milliliters of a 15% acid and 85% water mix. Does the chemist need more of the 10% acid and 90% water mix than the 30% acid and 70% water mix to make this new mix? *Explain.*

Chapter 7 Systems of Equations and Inequalities

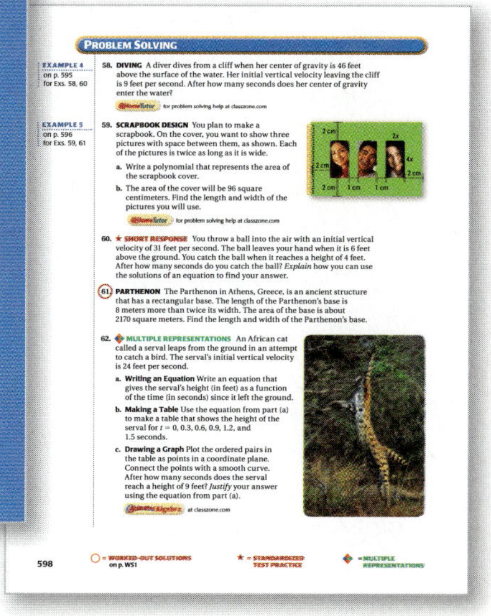

PROBLEM SOLVING

EXAMPLE 4 on p. 595 for Exs. 58, 60

58. DIVING A diver dives from a cliff when her center of gravity is 46 feet above the surface of the water. Her initial vertical velocity leaving the cliff is 9 feet per second. After how many seconds does her center of gravity enter the water?

    @HomeTutor for problem solving help at classzone.com

EXAMPLE 5 on p. 596 for Exs. 59, 61

59. SCRAPBOOK DESIGN You plan to make a scrapbook. On the cover, you want to show three pictures with space between them, as shown. Each of the pictures is twice as long as it is wide.
    a. Write a polynomial that represents the area of the scrapbook cover.
    b. The area of the cover will be 96 square centimeters. Find the length and width of the pictures you will use.

    @HomeTutor for problem solving help at classzone.com

60. ★ SHORT RESPONSE You throw a ball into the air with an initial vertical velocity of 31 feet per second. The ball leaves your hand when it is 6 feet above the ground. You catch the ball when it reaches a height of 4 feet. After how many seconds do you catch the ball? *Explain* how you can use the solutions of an equation to find your answer.
61. PARTHENON The Parthenon in Athens, Greece, is an ancient structure that has a rectangular base. The length of the Parthenon's base is 8 meters more than twice its width. The area of the base is about 2170 square meters. Find the length and width of the Parthenon's base.
62. MULTIPLE REPRESENTATIONS An African cat called a serval leaps from the ground in an attempt to catch a bird. The serval's initial vertical velocity is 24 feet per second.
    a. **Writing an Equation** Write an equation that gives the serval's height (in feet) as a function of the time (in seconds) since it left the ground.
    b. **Making a Table** Use the equation from part (a) to make a table that shows the height of the serval for $t = 0, 0.3, 0.6, 0.9, 1.2$, and 1.5 seconds.
    c. **Drawing a Graph** Plot the ordered pairs in the table as points in a coordinate plane. Connect the points with a smooth curve. After how many seconds does the serval reach a height of 9 feet? *Justify* your answer using the equation from part (a).

    Animated Algebra at classzone.com

598

○ = WORKED-OUT SOLUTIONS on p. WS1 ★ = STANDARDIZED TEST PRACTICE ◆ = MULTIPLE REPRESENTATIONS

10.6A Use a Simulation to Test an Assumption

MATERIALS · coins · graphing calculator

QUESTION   **How do you determine whether a coin is fair?**

How do you know if a coin is "fair"? That is, when you flip it, how do you know a coin is equally likely to land heads or tails?

You can flip an actual coin many times to help you decide whether you think it's fair. But what kinds of seemingly "unusual" outcomes might occur even with a fair coin? How do you know what you can expect?

In this activity, you will perform physical experiments with a coin and also use *simulation* with a graphing calculator to model flipping a coin. The simulation lets you quickly repeat an event with two equally likely outcomes to compare with results that you might get from an actual coin.

EXPLORE 1   **Perform an experiment**

A friend gives you a coin. You flip it 4 times, and you get tails all 4 times. Would you feel confident in concluding that the coin is not fair?

STEP 1 *Flip coins*

Working in pairs, flip a coin 4 times. Repeat this experiment a total of 10 times, so that you have 10 trials of 4 flips. Record your results in a table like the one shown. Count the number of trials that fall into each of these categories: 4 heads, 3 heads and 1 tails, 2 heads and 2 tails, 1 heads and 3 tails, 4 tails.

	Flip 1	Flip 2	Flip 3	Flip 4
Trial 1	?	?	?	?
Trial 2	?	?	?	?

STEP 2 *Display results*

Collect all of the data generated by the pairs of students in your class. Combine the outcomes for all of the trials, and then display the class data using a bar graph set up like the one at the right.

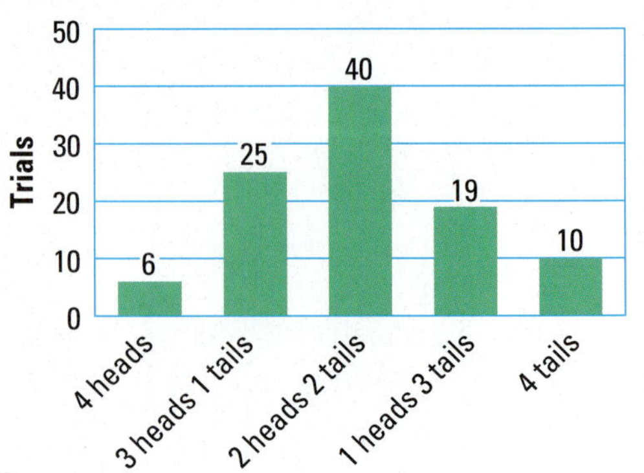

STEP 3 *Analyze results*

What outcome or outcomes occurred the most frequently? How many times did 4 heads or 4 tails occur? Would you be reasonably certain concluding that the coin your friend gave you is not fair? *Explain.*

A friend gives you a coin. You flip it 7 times, and you get tails all 7 times. Would you feel confident in concluding that the coin is not fair?

STEP 1 *Generate data*

For the simulation, let 0 represent flipping heads and let 1 represent flipping tails. On a graphing calculator, press the **MATH** key, select the "PRB" menu, and choose "randInt(." Perform the keystrokes for "randInt(0, 1, 7)" and press **ENTER**. The calculator will produce a list of seven digits (0 or 1) at random, as shown, where the outcomes 0 and 1 are equally likely to occur.

Press **ENTER** 20 times to obtain 20 lists of 7 "coin flips." Keep a tally to record the number of these 20 trials whose results fall into each of these categories: 7 heads, 6 heads and 1 tail, 5 heads and 2 tails, ..., 1 heads and 6 tails, 7 tails.

STEP 2 *Display results*

Collect all of the data generated by the pairs in your class. Combine the outcomes for all of the trials and display the class data using a bar graph similar to the one used in Explore 1. It will have 8 bars.

STEP 3 *Analyze results*

What outcome or outcomes occurred the most? How many times did 7 heads or 7 tails occur? Would you be reasonably certain concluding that the coin your friend gave you is not fair? *Explain.*

1. In Explore 1, find the theoretical probability of flipping 4 tails in a row. Does this affect your confidence in the coin's fairness or unfairness? *Explain.*

2. In Explore 2, find the theoretical probability of flipping 7 tails in a row. Does this affect your confidence in the coin's fairness or unfairness? *Explain.*

3. A simulation of flipping a coin 5 times in a row is performed 200 times. The results of the simulation are shown in the table below.

	5 heads 0 tails	4 heads 1 tails	3 heads 2 tails	2 heads 3 tails	1 heads 4 tails	0 heads 5 tails
Outcomes	1	5	27	61	72	34

   a. Make a bar graph of the data.

   b. Do you think that the simulation represents a coin that is fair or not fair? *Explain.*

Mastering *the* Standards

for Mathematical Practice

The topics described in the Standards for Mathematical Content will vary from year to year. However, the *way* in which you learn, study, and think about mathematics will not. The Standards for Mathematical Practice describe skills that you will use in all of your math courses.

Mathematical Practices

1. *Make sense of problems and persevere in solving them.*
2. *Reason abstractly and quantitatively.*
3. *Construct viable arguments and critique the reasoning of others.*
4. *Model with mathematics.*
5. *Use appropriate tools strategically.*
6. *Attend to precision.*
7. *Look for and make use of structure.*
8. *Look for and express regularity in repeated reasoning.*

⑤ Use appropriate tools strategically.

Mathematically proficient students consider the available tools when solving a... problem... [and] are... able to use technological tools to explore and deepen their understanding...

In your book

Problem Solving Workshops explore alternative methods as tools for problem solving. A variety of **Activities** use concrete and technological tools to explore mathematical concepts.

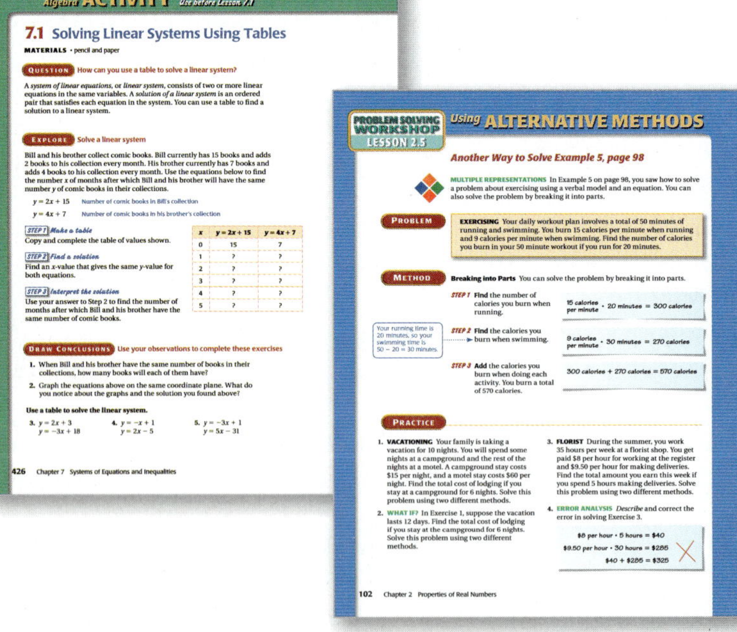

11.3A Investigate the Shapes of Data Distributions

MATERIALS • graph paper • graphing calculator

QUESTION How do you describe and interpret data distributions with various shapes?

A histogram of data can have different shapes. It may be symmetrical or not, may be bell-shaped or not, or may have a long "tail" in one direction. It may have no recognizable shape. There are recurring patterns in data distributions, however, that let you predict probabilities involving data values.

EXPLORE 1 Simulate rolling a die repeatedly until you get a 5

STEP 1 *Perform a simulation*

Press **MATH**, then select "PRB," then "randInt(." The command randInt(1, 6) gives a random integer from 1 to 6 when you press **ENTER**. The screen shows 6 results.

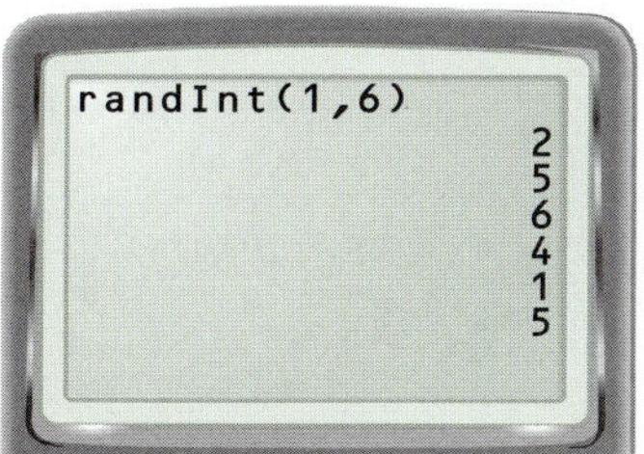

STEP 2 *Make a plot*

In Step 1, a "5" first appears in the 2nd trial. It takes 4 more trials to get the next "5." These two results are shown below. Make a similar plot for your data. Plot 40 or 50 results.

Number of trials to get a 5

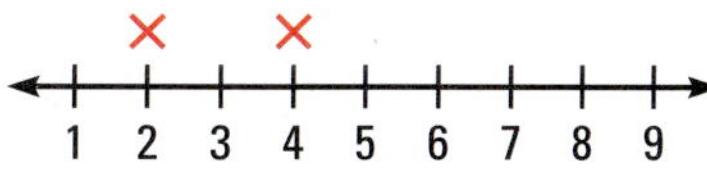

STEP 3 *Observe and compare*

Describe your plot. Include the following.

- What is the general shape?
- Is it symmetric?
- Does it have a clear "middle?"

Compare your plot with those of other groups. Were their results similar?

What was the greatest number of rolls required by any single group to get a 5?

EXPLORE 2 Simulate rolling a die 100 times

STEP 1 *Perform a simulation*

To simulate 100 rolls of a die, you can perform all 100 "rolls" at once and store the results in a list by entering the command below.

randInt(1, 6, 100) **STO ▶** **2nd** [L1]

Pressing **ENTER** displays the list on the home screen and enters it in the Statistics memory.

STEP 2 *Make a histogram*

Press **2nd** [Stat Plot], turn on Plot1, and select the histogram icon. Set "Xlist" to L1 and "Freq" to 1. Enter the window below, then press **GRAPH**.

STEP 3 *Observe and compare*

Describe your plot and compare plots as you did in Step 3 above.

You can very quickly make a new plot:

Press **2nd** [QUIT] to return to the home screen. Press **ENTER** to produce a new list. Then press **GRAPH**. Do this a few times. How does the graph change?

STEP 1 Perform a simulation

Enter randInt(1, 6, 10) and press **ENTER** to simulate rolling 10 dice. Below you can see three "dice" that display even results. (To see the last three results in the list, scroll to the right.)

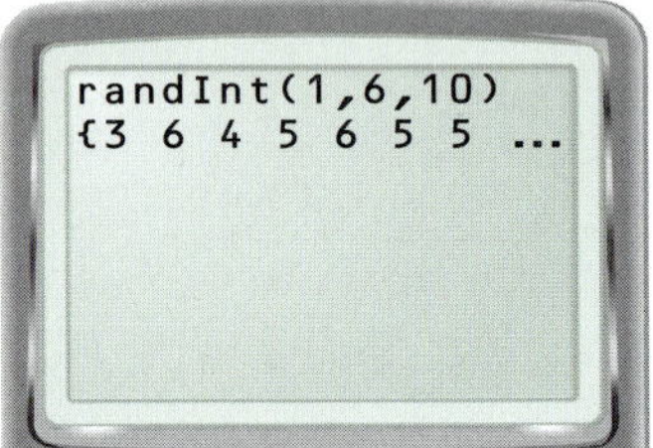

STEP 2 Make a plot

Press **ENTER**, count the number of even numbers in the new list, and record it in a plot like the one below, which shows results for 10 rolls of 10 dice. Repeat as many times as time allows.

Even numbers rolled

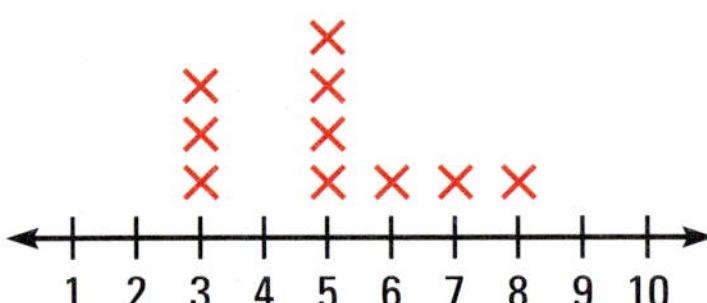

STEP 3 Observe and compare

Describe your plot and compare plots as you did in Explore 1 and 2.

How does the shape of this plot compare with the shapes of the plots from Explore 1 and 2?

EXPLORE 4   Combine data

STEP 1 Combine results from Explore 1 Combine the results of all groups to make a class histogram. Compare your plot and the class histogram.

STEP 2 Simulate combining results from Explore 2 To simulate combining results from Explore 2 for 10 groups, repeat the first two steps of Explore 2, but use the command randInt(1, 6, 999). (Note that 999 is the largest number the calculator allows.) Also, change the viewing window to Ymin = −50, Ymax = 250, and Yscl = 50. Compare your histogram and the class histogram.

STEP 3 Combine results from Explore 3 Combine the results of all groups to make a class histogram. Compare your plot and the class histogram.

DRAW CONCLUSIONS   Use your observations to complete these exercises

1. Did the graphs in each Explore have similar or very different shapes? *Explain.*

2. For each Explore, how did combining the results of the groups into one graph change the shapes? Predict what you think the shape of each histogram might be if you could repeat each simulation thousands of times.

3. Symmetric, bell-shaped data distributions, such as the one at the right, occur frequently in real world models. This curve has special properties that make it extremely useful for finding probabilities. Which of the Explore results most closely resembles a curve with this shape?

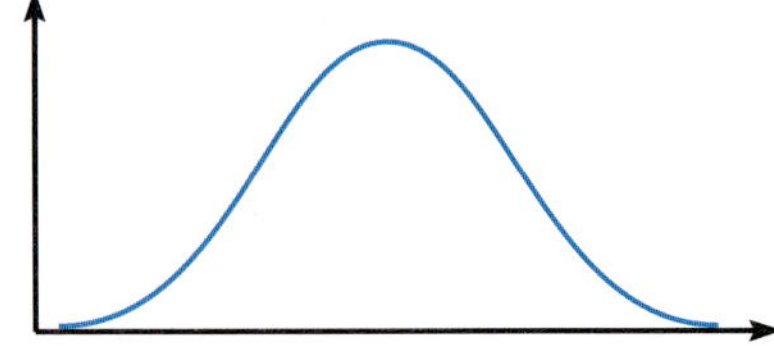

11.3B Find the Area Under a Normal Curve

QUESTION How can you use a graphing calculator to find the area under a normal curve?

EXAMPLE 1 Find a normal probability

The lengths of a group of newborn babies are normally distributed with a mean of 19.8 inches and a standard deviation of 1.6 inches. Find the probability that a randomly chosen baby in this group is at most 20.5 inches long.

STEP 1 *Clarify the problem* We want to find $P(x \le 20.5)$ for a normal distribution with a mean of 19.8 and a standard deviation of 1.6.

STEP 2 *Enter information* Access the "Distributions" menu by pressing [2nd] [VARS]. Select "normalcdf(," then enter (lower bound, upper bound, mean, standard deviation). Use 0 as the lower bound. You can see at the right that the probability is about 66.9%.

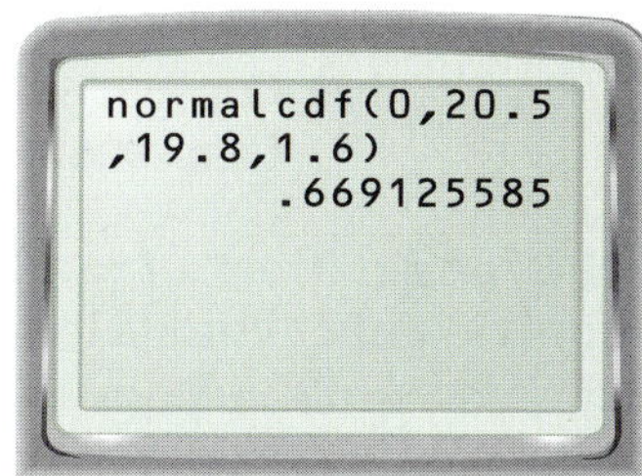

EXAMPLE 2 Find and display an area under a normal curve

Find $P(19 \le x \le 22)$ for the situation in Example 1.

STEP 1 *Enter information* In the Distributions menu, select "DRAW" at the top and then "ShadeNorm(." You must enter (lower bound, upper bound, mean, standard deviation). Enter 19 for the lower bound and 22 for the upper bound. Do not yet press [ENTER].

STEP 2 *Choose a viewing window* For a window that shows about 3 standard deviations to either side of the mean, let Xmin = 15 and Xmax = 25. The area under the curve is 1, so the maximum Y-value will be well less than 1. Let Ymin = −0.075 and Ymax = 0.25. Return to the home screen and press [ENTER]. You can see at the right that the area is about 0.607, so the probability is about 60.7%.

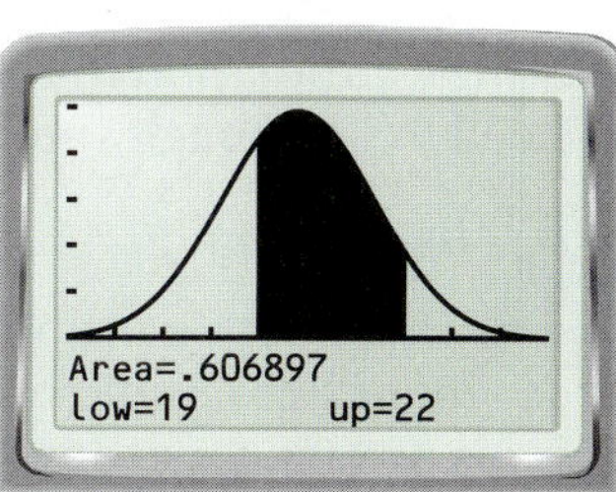

PRACTICE

1. The mean number of potatoes per 15 pound bag from a supplier is 42, with a standard deviation of 4.5. The distribution is normal. Find the probability that a randomly selected bag contains the given number of potatoes.

   a. 50 or fewer   b. at least 35   c. 37 to 47   d. 40 to 44

2. Scores on a qualifying exam are normally distributed with a mean score of 230 and a standard deviation of 43. A score of 250 is required to pass.

   a. Find and display the area under the normal curve for passing scores.

   b. Find and display the area under the normal curve for scores of 200−250. (*Note:* You will first need to clear the drawing from part (a).)

11.4A Estimate a Population Proportion

MATERIALS · graphing calculator

QUESTION How can you use a sample proportion to estimate a population proportion?

You can use statistics to make reasonable predictions, or *inferences*, about an entire population from a sample of the population. A *population proportion* is the ratio of members of a population with a particular characteristic to total members of the population. A *sample proportion* is the ratio of members of a sample of the population with a particular characteristic to total members of the sample.

EXPLORE 1 Compare sample proportions from a population with known proportion

In the "population" of randomly-generated decimals between 0 and 1, the proportion of decimals less than 0.6 is 0.6. Simulate random samples of decimals from this population, and compare the sample proportions with the population proportion.

STEP 1 *Perform a simulation*

Use a graphing calculator to generate 40 random decimals between 0 and 1. Press **MATH**, choose the "PRB" menu, select "rand," and press **ENTER**. The display will be similar to the one at the right.

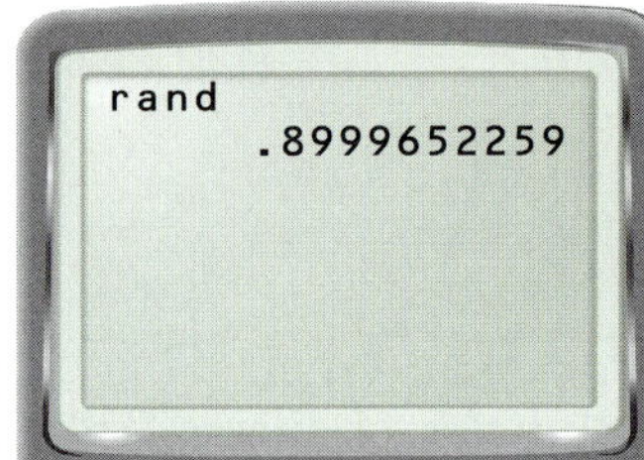

Press **ENTER** 40 times to generate 40 random numbers. Keep a tally of the number of decimals below 0.6. Then find your sample proportion by dividing the number of decimals below 0.6—the "successes"—by the number of trials, which is 40.

Repeat the simulation to find another sample proportion. Each group will need to do enough simulations so that there are 40 in all for the class.

STEP 2 *Display sample proportions*

Collect all 40 sample proportions. Make a histogram of the sample proportions using intervals of 0.05, for example, [0.55, 0.6). The histogram for one set of 40 sample proportions is shown at the right.

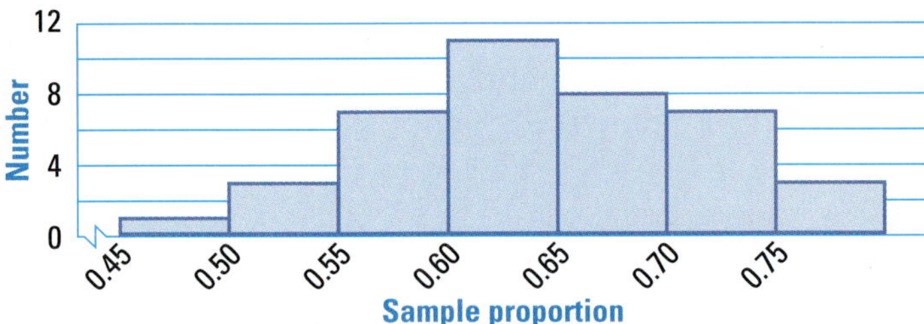

STEP 3 *Investigate sample proportions*

Exclude the single smallest and single greatest of the 40 sample proportions. Then find the interval that contains the remaining 38 sample proportions.

Plot the interval containing the middle 38 sample proportions as shown. The blue horizontal segment represents the middle 38 of 40, or 95%, of the sample proportions. So, 95% of the time, the sample proportion from the simulation fell within the interval graphed.

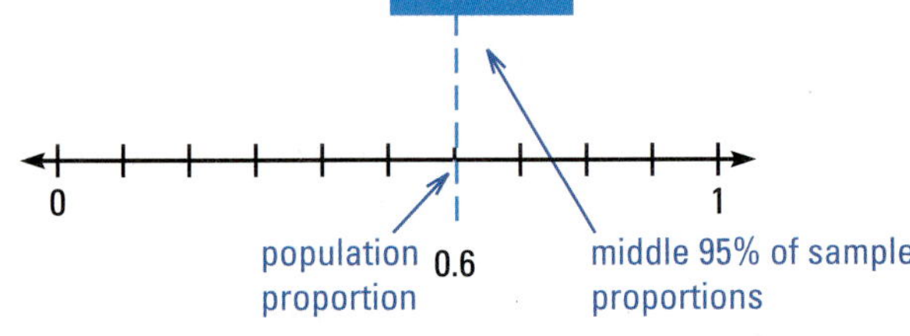

 Estimate a population proportion from a sample proportion

STEP 1 *Investigate sample proportions*

There are formulas for calculating intervals expected to contain 95% of the sample proportions given any population proportion and sample size. The chart at the right shows the 95% sample proportion intervals for population proportions of 0.05, 0.1, 0.15, ..., 0.9, 0.95 where the sample size is $n = 40$.

The interval in red is the calculated 95% sample proportion interval for a population proportion of 0.6. Compare this interval with the 95% interval your class created for the simulation in Explore 1.

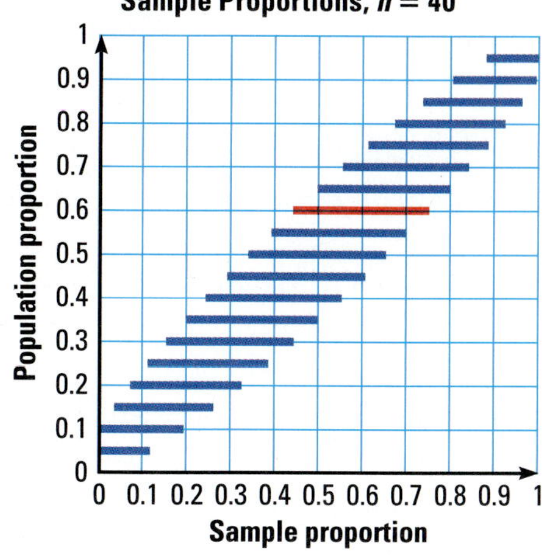

STEP 2 *Use a sample proportion*

It's not usually possible to collect data for entire populations. So, data from samples are used to estimate unknown population proportions. Suppose you want to estimate a population proportion using a sample of size 40, and your sample has a sample proportion of 0.6. Which populations are most likely to have produced a sample like yours?

The green vertical line shown at right highlights a sample proportion of 0.6. Any horizontal bar that this line touches corresponds to a population that will produce a sample whose sample proportion lies within that bar 95% of the time. The green line touches the bars for population proportions of 0.45 up to 0.75. So, *if we have a sample of size 40 with a sample proportion of 0.6, then, 95% of the time, the population proportion should lie in the interval from 0.45 to 0.75.*

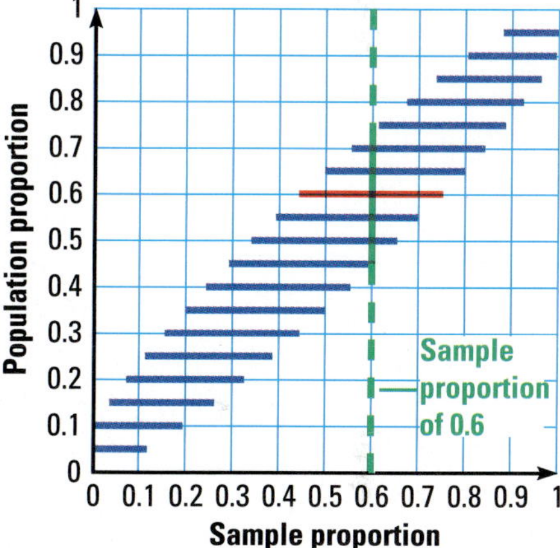

STEP 3 *Estimate a population proportion*

For a sample of size 40 with sample proportion 0.3, use the chart to estimate the interval that contains the corresponding population proportion 95% of the time.

DRAW CONCLUSIONS **Use your observations to complete these exercises**

1. As a class, repeat Steps 1 and 2 of Explore 1, but with each trial count the number of decimals less than 0.6 out of *80* random decimals. *Describe* how increasing the sample size in each trial affects the shape of the histogram.

2. You have used the *margin of error* $\pm \dfrac{1}{\sqrt{n}}$ for a sample of size n to estimate an interval containing a population proportion. More precisely, this expression is $\pm 2\sqrt{\dfrac{\hat{p}(1 - \hat{p})}{n}}$, where the symbol $\hat{p}$ (read as "p-hat") is the sample proportion. Then $\hat{p} - 2\sqrt{\dfrac{\hat{p}(1 - \hat{p})}{n}} < p < \hat{p} + 2\sqrt{\dfrac{\hat{p}(1 - \hat{p})}{n}}$ is a 95% *confidence interval* for the population proportion p. We can expect the population proportion to be in this interval 95% of the time. Find a 95% confidence interval for the population proportion for a sample of size 150 with a sample proportion of 0.8.

11.5A Compare Surveys, Experiments, and Observational Studies

Before	You studied sampling methods for collecting data using a survey.
Now	You will learn how studies are used to collect data.
Why	So you can design a study to collect data, as in Ex. 16.

Key Vocabulary
- **biased questions**
- **experiment**
- **observational study**
- **controlled experiment**
- **control group**
- **treatment group**
- **randomized comparative experiment**

SURVEYS Previously, you learned that in choosing a sample of a population to survey, you should do your best to select an unbiased sample to help ensure that the survey data represent the population. Random samples are preferred since they are less likely to be biased.

In designing a survey, it is also very important to word survey questions carefully. Answers to poorly worded questions may not accurately reflect the opinions or actions of those being surveyed. Questions that are flawed in a way that leads to inaccurate results are called **biased questions**. Questions may be biased in several ways:

- The wording of the question may encourage or pressure the respondent to answer in a particular way.
- The question may be perceived as too sensitive to answer truthfully.
- The question may not provide the respondent with enough information to give an accurate opinion.

Bias may also be introduced in survey questioning in other ways, such as by the order in which questions are asked or by respondents giving answers they believe will please the questioner.

EXAMPLE 1 Identify and correct bias in survey questioning

Tell why the question may be biased or otherwise introduce bias into the survey. Describe a way to correct the flaw.

a.

b.

Solution

a. This question assumes that the respondent is familiar with the proposal. To get accurate results that lead to valid conclusions, state the proposal clearly using neutral language before asking the question.

b. Patients who brush less than twice per day or do not floss daily may be afraid to admit this since the dentist is asking the question. One improvement would be to have patients answer questions about dental hygiene on paper and put the paper anonymously into a box.

EXPERIMENTS AND OBSERVATIONAL STUDIES You have seen that surveys are one way to collect data, but different situations and purposes require different data gathering techniques. For example, many studies are designed to try to determine whether a quantity that varies can be associated with measured differences in two different groups of individuals.

An **experiment** imposes a treatment on individuals in order to collect data on their response to the treatment. The treatment may be a medical treatment, or it can be any action that might affect a variable in the experiment, such as adding methanol to gasoline and then measuring its effect on fuel efficiency.

In some cases, it may be difficult to control or isolate the variable being studied, or it may be unethical to subject people to a certain treatment or to withhold it from them. In this case, an *observational study* is used. An **observational study** observes individuals and measures variables without controlling the individuals or their environment.

EXAMPLE 2 Identify experiments and observational studies

Determine whether each situation is an example of an experiment or an observational study. Explain.

a. A researcher asks college students how many hours of sleep they get on an average night and examines whether the number of hours of sleep affects students' grades.

b. A Parks Department employee wants to know if latex paint is more durable than non-latex paint. She has 50 park benches painted with latex paint and has 50 park benches painted with non-latex paint.

Solution

a. The researcher gathers data without controlling the individuals or applying a treatment. The situation is an observational study.

b. A treatment (painting benches with latex paint) is applied to some of the individuals (benches) in the study. The situation is an experiment.

GUIDED PRACTICE for Examples 1 and 2

1. Tell whether the survey question below may be biased or otherwise introduce bias into the survey. *Explain.*

"Do you, like most people your age, enjoy watching the latest music videos?"

2. Determine whether the situation described in the research summary shown at the right is an example of an experiment or an observational study. *Explain.*

> **…TECH NOTES…**
>
> **A Faster Web Site**
>
> To test the redesign of its Web site, an online bookseller assembled 96 users of the site and randomly divided them into two groups. One group used the new Web site to make an online purchase and one group used the old Web site to do the same transaction. Users of the new site were able to complete the purchase 22% faster.

 In a **controlled experiment**, two groups are studied under identical conditions with the exception of one variable. The group under ordinary conditions is the **control group**. The group that is subjected to the treatment is the **treatment group**.

In a **randomized comparative experiment**, individuals are randomly assigned to the control group or the treatment group. The comparison of the control group and the treatment group makes it possible to determine any effects of the treatment.

Randomization minimizes bias and produces groups of individuals that are theoretically similar in all ways before the treatment is applied. Conclusions drawn from an experiment that is not a randomized comparative experiment may not be valid.

EXAMPLE 3   Evaluate a published report

Determine whether the study described in the health bulletin below is a randomized comparative experiment. If it is, describe the treatment, the treatment group, and the control group. If it is not, explain why not and discuss whether the conclusions drawn from the study are valid.

> ### Health Watch!
>
> **Milk Fights Cavities**
>
> At Ashland Middle School, students were given the choice of drinking milk or other beverages at lunch. Fifty students who chose milk were monitored for one year, as were 50 students who chose other beverages. At the end of the year, students in the "milk" group had 15% fewer cavities than students in the other group.

Solution

The study is not a randomized comparative experiment because the individuals were not randomly assigned to a control group and a treatment group. (In fact, the study is an observational study, not an experiment, since no treatment is imposed.)

The study's conclusion that milk fights cavities may or may not be valid. There may be other reasons why students who chose milk had fewer cavities. For example, students who voluntarily choose milk at lunch may be more likely to have other healthy eating or dental care habits that could affect the number of cavities they have.

GUIDED PRACTICE   for Example 3

3. Determine whether the study described in the research summary for Guided Practice Exercise 2 is a randomized comparative experiment. If it is, describe the treatment, the treatment group, and the control group. If it is not, explain why not and discuss whether the conclusions drawn from the study are valid.

WELL-DESIGNED STUDIES Randomization is a key element of well-designed studies. How randomization applies to different kinds of studies varies, as shown below.

Sample survey	Observational study	Experiment
A random sample is selected to be surveyed from the population studied.	As possible, random samples can be selected for the groups being studied.	Individuals are assigned at random to the treatment group or the control group.

Surveys do not compare groups, and so do not address cause and effect. Good observational studies and experiments are designed to be comparative—to compare data from two or more groups looking for a relationship between variables. But only a well-designed experiment can determine a cause-and-effect relationship.

Comparative Studies and Causality

- An observational study can identify *correlation* between variables, but not *causality*. Variables other than what is being measured may be affecting the results. For example, vigorous exercise in older people correlates with longer life, but comparing groups only on exercise and lifespan ignores other factors, such as that people who are unhealthy to begin with may not be able to exercise vigorously.

- A rigorous randomized comparative experiment, by eliminating sources of variation other than the controlled variable, can make valid cause-and-effect conclusions possible.

EXAMPLE 4   **Design an experiment or observational study**

Explain whether the following research topic is best investigated through an experiment or an observational study. Then explain how you would design the experiment or observational study.

You want to know if listening to music using earphones for more than one hour per day affects a person's hearing.

Solution

The treatment (listening to music using earphones for more than one hour a day) may affect an individual's hearing, so it is not ethical to assign individuals to a control or treatment group. Use an observational study.

Randomly choose one group of individuals who already listen to music using earphones for more than one hour per day.

Randomly choose one group of individuals who do not listen to music using earphones for more than one hour per day.

Monitor the hearing of the individuals in both groups at regular intervals.

11.5A EXERCISES

SKILL PRACTICE

1. **VOCABULARY** Copy and complete: An __?__ observes individuals and measures variables without controlling the individuals or their environment.

2. ★ **WRITING** *Describe* the difference between an experiment and an observational study.

EXAMPLE 1
on p. CC36
for Exs. 3–6

IDENTIFYING BIASED SURVEY QUESTIONS **Tell why the question may be biased or otherwise introduce bias into the survey. Describe a way to correct the flaw.**

3. "Do you agree with all of the budget cuts proposed by the mayor?"

4. "Would you rather watch the latest award-winning movie or just read some book?"

5. "The tap water coming from our western water supply contains twice the level of arsenic of water from our eastern supply. Do you think the government should address this health problem?"

6. A child with an adult asks, "Will you vote for our school bond issue?"

EXAMPLE 2
on p. CC37
for Exs. 7–9

CLASSIFYING STUDIES **Determine whether each situation is an example of an *experiment* or an *observational study*. Explain.**

7. A researcher compares incomes of people who live in rural areas with incomes of people who live in large cities.

8. A farmer wants to know if a new fertilizer affects the weight of the fruit produced by strawberry plants. She applies the fertilizer to 10 rows of plants and does not apply the fertilizer to 10 other rows of plants.

9. ★ **MULTIPLE CHOICE** A doctor studies the effects of nicotine on a person's health by monitoring the health of 100 randomly selected smokers and 100 randomly selected nonsmokers. This is an example of what type of study?

   A experiment   **B** observational study

   C sample survey   **D** none of the above

EXAMPLE 3
on p. CC38
for Exs. 10, 11

ERROR ANALYSIS *Describe* and correct the error in describing the study given below.

A company's researchers want to study the effects of adding shea butter to their existing hair conditioner. They monitor the hair quality of 50 randomly selected volunteers using the old conditioner and 50 randomly selected volunteers using the new shea butter conditioner.

10. The control group is volunteers who do not use either of the conditioners. ✗

11. The study is a comparative observational study. ✗

12. **CHALLENGE** *Explain* why observational studies, rather than experiments, are usually used in astronomy.

EXAMPLE 4
on p. CC39
for Exs. 13–15

Explain whether the research topic is best addressed through an *experiment* or an *observational study*. Then explain how you would design the experiment or the observational study.

13. You want to know if homes that are close to parks or schools have higher property values than other homes.

14. You want to know if flowers sprayed twice a day with a mist of water stay fresh longer than flowers that are not sprayed.

15. Determine whether the study described in the report is a randomized comparative experiment. If it is, describe the treatment, the treatment group, and the control group. If it is not, explain why not and discuss whether the conclusions drawn from the study are valid.

> **Early Birds Make Better Drivers**
>
> A recent study shows that adults who rise before 6:30 A.M. are better drivers than other adults. The study monitored the driving records of 140 volunteers who always wake up before 6:30 and 140 volunteers who never wake up before 6:30. The early risers had 12% fewer accidents.

16. Describe how you would set up a randomized, controlled experiment to investigate the hypothesis below. Include any precautions you would take to ensure that your conclusions are valid.

    Dog food with added Omega-3 fatty acids will give dogs a shiny coat.

17. ★ **WRITING** *Explain* why a randomized comparative experiment should be used to collect data whenever possible.

18. **MEDICINE** A researcher studied the effect of fiber supplements on heart disease. She identified 175 people who take fiber supplements and 175 people who do not take fiber supplements. She found that those who took the supplements had 19% fewer heart attacks those who did not. She concluded that taking fiber supplements reduces the incidence of heart attacks.

    a. *Explain* why the researcher's conclusion may not be valid.

    b. *Describe* how the researcher could have conducted the study differently to produce valid results.

19. **CHALLENGE** Will replicating an experiment on many individuals produce data that is more likely to accurately represent a population than performing the experiment only once? *Explain.*

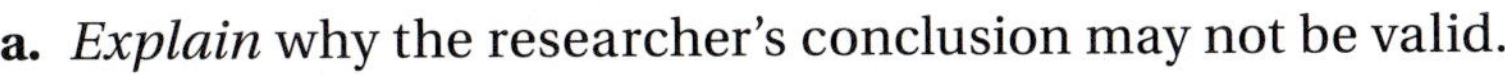

Graph the function.

PREVIEW
Prepare for
Lesson 11.5 in
Exs. 20–22.

20. $y = 2x - 1$ *(Lesson 2.3)*

21. $y = x^2 - 2x - 3$ *(Lesson 4.1)*

22. **EMPLOYMENT** In one month, you earned $286 working a total of 34 hours at two jobs. You earn $7 per hour baby-sitting and $9 per hour working at a retail store. How many hours did you work? *(Lesson 3.2)*

11.5B Simulate an Experimental Difference

MATERIALS • index cards • scissors • small paper bag • graphing calculator

QUESTION How can you test a hypothesis about an experiment?

When you perform a randomized comparative experiment and measure a difference between the control and treatment groups, how do you know if the difference is from the treatment or if it's just a chance result of the choice of the groups? One way is to *resample*: combine all the measurements from both groups, and repeatedly create new "control" and "treatment" groups at random from the measurements. Then see how often you get chance differences between the new groups that are at least as large as the one you measured.

EXPLORE 1 Resample data

A randomized experiment tests whether a soil supplement affects the total yield (in kilograms) of cherry tomato plants. The table below shows the results. How does the difference in the means of the control and treatment groups compare with differences resulting from chance?

Total Yield of Tomato Plants (kilograms)									
Control group	1.4	0.9	1.2	1.3	2.0	1.2	0.7	1.9	1.4	1.7
Treatment group	1.4	0.9	1.5	1.8	1.6	1.8	2.4	1.9	1.9	1.7

STEP 1 *Calculate means* Find the mean yield of the control group, $\overline{x}_{control}$, and the mean yield of the treatment group, $\overline{x}_{treatment}$. Then find the difference $\overline{x}_{treatment} - \overline{x}_{control}$. Note that the difference can be positive or negative, and is 0 when $\overline{x}_{treatment} = \overline{x}_{control}$.

STEP 2 *Combine measurements and resample* Working in pairs, cut index cards to make 20 equal-sized pieces, and write one yield measurement on each. Place the pieces in a bag, shake, and randomly choose 10. Call this the "treatment" group, and call the 10 pieces in the bag the "control" group. Find the mean for each group, record $\overline{x}_{treatment} - \overline{x}_{control}$, and return the pieces to the bag.

Perform the resampling experiment 5 times, each time finding the difference of means. Sample results for 5 resamplings made by each of two pairs of students are shown at the right.

$\overline{x}_{treatment} - \overline{x}_{control}$:

Pair 1: -0.28, -0.24, -0.18, -0.12, 0.30

Pair 2: -0.26, 0.00, 0.12, 0.18, 0.28

STEP 3 *State the null hypothesis* The *null hypothesis* is the assumption that measured differences between a treatment group and a control group are a result of chance. The null hypothesis for this activity is the following:

The soil nutrient has no effect on the yield of the cherry tomato plants.

To conclude that the treatment *is* responsible for the difference in yield, you need strong evidence to *reject* the null hypothesis. To evaluate the null hypothesis, compare the experimental difference of means with the resampling differences.

STEP 1 *Collect and display results* Collect all the differences $\overline{x}_{treatment} - \overline{x}_{control}$ calculated by pairs of students in the class in Explore 1. Display the differences in a histogram. A sample histogram for 50 resamplings made using a graphing calculator and an interval for the difference of means of 0.05 is shown at the right.

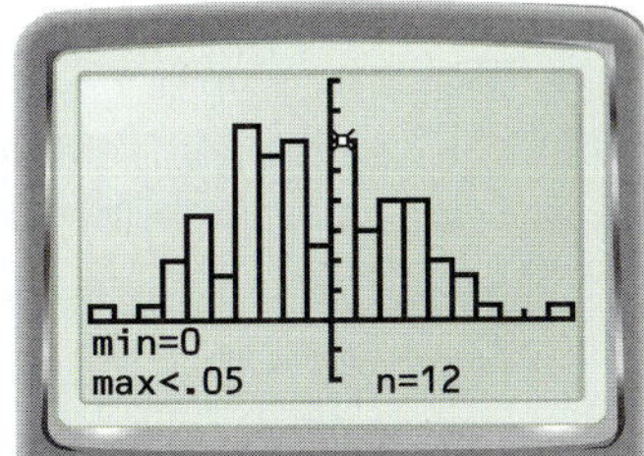

STEP 2 *Analyze resampling data* In Step 1 of Explore 1, you calculated the experimental difference of means. Draw a vertical line on your class histogram to represent this difference.

If the experimental difference of means lies in one of the tails of the resampling distribution, then resampling gave a difference of means at least as large as the experimental difference only rarely. This gives evidence for rejecting the null hypothesis. More specifically, the following are true:

- If the experimental difference of means falls outside of the middle 90% of the resampling differences of means, you can reject the null hypothesis at the 90% confidence level.

- If the experimental difference of means falls outside of the middle 95% of the resampling differences of means, you can reject the null hypothesis at the 95% confidence level.

STEP 3 *Evaluate results* Is your class able to reject the null hypothesis? *Explain*. What does this mean regarding the original experiment?

DRAW CONCLUSIONS Use your observations to complete these exercises

1. Find the mean of all of the resampling differences of means collected by all pairs of students in Step 1 of Explore 2. This mean should approximate the most likely result when the null hypothesis is true. Is the mean of the resampling differences of means for your class close to this value?

2. In Explore 1, how many resampling choices for the treatment and control groups are theoretically possible? Suppose that a computer is programmed to generate all possible control and treatment group assignments, to find the differences of means, and then to draw a histogram of the results. Would you prefer to make conclusions about the experiment using the histogram from the computer or the histogram for your class? *Explain*.

3. Suppose the company that produces the soil nutrient featured in the experiment described in Explore 1 advertises that growing tomato plants in soil enriched with the nutrient will increase the yield of the tomato plants. Is this an accurate statement? *Explain*.

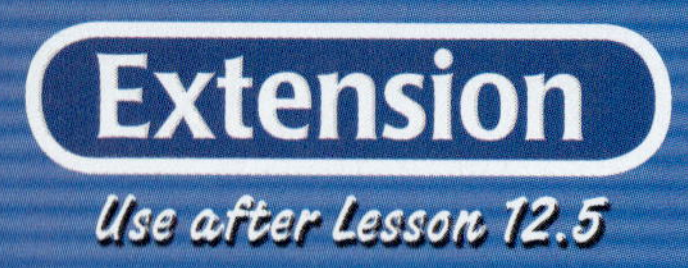

Translate Between Recursive and Explicit Rules for Sequences

GOAL Translate between recursive and explicit rules for arithmetic and geometric sequences.

The box below summarizes the recursive and explicit rules for arithmetic sequences with common difference d, and for geometric sequences with common ratio r.

KEY CONCEPT *For Your Notebook*

Sequence Formulas

Recursive Formulas

Arithmetic sequence: $a_n = a_{n-1} + d$

Geometric sequence: $a_n = r \cdot a_{n-1}$

Explicit Formulas

Arithmetic sequence: $a_n = a_1 + (n-1)d$

Geometric sequence: $a_n = a_1 r^{n-1}$

To translate from an explicit rule to a recursive rule for an arithmetic sequence, find the first term a_1 and the common difference d. To translate from an explicit rule to a recursive rule for a geometric sequence, find a_1 and the common ratio r.

EXAMPLE 1 **Translate from an explicit rule to a recursive rule**

Write a recursive rule for the sequence.

a. $a_n = -6 + 8n$

b. $a_n = -3\left(\frac{1}{2}\right)^{n-1}$

Solution

a. $a_n = -6 + 8n$ Write explicit rule.

$a_1 = -6 + 8(1) = 2$ Substitute 1 for n.

$d = 8$ The coefficient of n is d.

$a_1 = 2,\ a_n = a_{n-1} + 8$ Write recursive rule.

b. $a_n = -3\left(\frac{1}{2}\right)^{n-1}$ Write explicit rule.

$a_1 = -3\left(\frac{1}{2}\right)^0 = -3$ Substitute 1 for n.

$r = \frac{1}{2}$ The common ratio is $\frac{1}{2}$.

$a_1 = -3,\ a_n = \frac{1}{2}a_{n-1}$ Write recursive rule.

To translate from a recursive rule to an explicit rule for an arithmetic sequence, find the common difference d. To translate from a recursive rule to an explicit rule for a geometric sequence, find the common ratio r.

EXAMPLE 2 Translate from a recursive rule to an explicit rule

Write an explicit rule for the sequence.

a. $a_1 = -5, a_n = a_{n-1} - 2$ **b.** $a_1 = 10, a_n = 2a_{n-1}$

Solution

a. $a_1 = -5, a_n = a_{n-1} - 2$ Write recursive rule.

$d = -2$ The number added or subtracted is d.

$a_n = -5 + (n-1)(-2)$ Substitute -5 for a_1 and -2 for d.

$a_n = -3 - 2n$ Write explicit rule.

b. $a_1 = 10, a_n = 2a_{n-1}$ Write recursive rule.

$r = 2$ The coefficient of a_{n-1} is r.

$a_n = 10(2)^{n-1}$ Substitute 10 for a_1 and 2 for r to write explicit rule.

PRACTICE

EXAMPLE 1
on p. CC44
for Exs. 1–4

Write a recursive rule for the sequence.

1. $a_n = 17 - 4n$

2. $a_n = 126 + 12.5n$

3. $a_n = 16(3)^{n-1}$

4. $a_n = 100{,}000(1.02)^{n-1}$

EXAMPLE 2
on p. CC45
for Exs. 5–8

Write an explicit rule for the sequence.

5. $a_1 = -12, a_n = a_{n-1} + 16$

6. $a_1 = 158, a_n = a_{n-1} - 7$

7. $a_1 = 2, a_n = -6a_{n-1}$

8. $a_1 = -\frac{1}{2}, a_n = 100a_{n-1}$

9. SAVINGS Juliana has saved \$82 so far to buy a bicycle. She saves an additional \$30 each month. The explicit rule $a_n = 30n + 82$ gives the amount saved after n months. Write a recursive rule for the amount Juliana has saved n months from now.

10. SOUP CANS A grocery store arranges cans in a pyramid-shaped display with 20 cans in the bottom row and 2 fewer cans in each subsequent row going up. The number of cans in each row is represented by the recursive rule $a_1 = 20, a_n = a_{n-1} - 2$. Write an explicit rule for the number of cans in row n.

11. SALARY Linda's salary is given by the explicit rule $a_n = 35{,}000(1.04)^{n-1}$, where n is the number of years she has worked. Write a recursive rule for her salary.

12. DEPRECIATION The value of Tim's car is given by the recursive rule $a_1 = 25{,}600$, $a_n = 0.86a_{n-1}$, where n is the number of years since Tim bought the car. Write an explicit rule for the value of Tim's car after n years.